CHORAL MUSICIANSHIP:
A Director's Guide to Better Singing

William C. Fenton & Sarah O. Johnson
First Edition

Library of Congress Catalog Card Number: 90–85675

ISBN 0-7935-9090-6

EXCLUSIVELY DISTRIBUTED BY

HAL•LEONARD®
CORPORATION

7777 W. BLUEMOUND RD. P.O. BOX 13819 MILWAUKEE, WI 53213

To all singers and choral directors who daily pursue the choral art, and to our students, past and present, who have inspired and taught us, this book is sincerely dedicated.

The writers would like to express their sincere gratitude to many friends and colleagues who were supportive during the preparation of this book. Special thanks are extended to Dr. Arthur Ostrander, Dean, School of Music, Ithaca College; and to Professor David Riley, Department of Music Education, Ithaca College, for his proof reading assistance; and to Dr. Hermann La Roux, Chairman, Voice Department, San Francisco Conservatory of Music

THE AUTHORS

WILLIAM C. FENTON is a Professor of Music in the School of Music at Ithaca College, Ithaca, New York, where he has also served as department chair in music education. Formerly, he was conductor of the University Chamber Singers at Wright State University, Dayton, Ohio. The Chamber Singers toured extensively including two concert tours in Europe. In addition, they performed throughout the state of Ohio and in the Mid-West, the South and the East.

A graduate of the Cincinnati Conservatory of Music (B. Mus., B. Sc.), he received a master's degree from Miami (Ohio) University and his doctorate from the University of Cincinnati.

Dr. Fenton is the author of a chapter on "Aspects of Religious Influence on Architecture, Painting and Music" in Teaching About Religion in the Public Schools, Argus Communications, 1977. Articles on music and specifically choral music have appeared in The Choral Journal, Triad (Ohio Music Education Association), and The School Music News (New York State School Music Association). He is listed in Who's Who and Who's Who in the Mid-West.

SARAH O. JOHNSON, mezzo-soprano soloist and teacher, has developed her private studio since moving to San Francisco, where she is also a member of a professional vocal quartet. She also is Director of Music at the First Presbyterian Church in San Anselmo and a choral clinician in the bay area. Formerly, she was Associate Professor of Music and department chair at Wright State University, Dayton, Ohio, and a teacher of voice and the pronunciation of foreign languages for singers. A graduate of Michigan State University (B. Mus.) and Kent State University (M. Mus.), she has also studied at the University of Cincinnati and in master classes at Indiana University, Juilliard School, Westminster Choir College, University of Maryland, and Trinity College, London, England.

She has sung extensively as a mezzo-soprano soloist in recital, oratorio and opera. Her teaching experience encompasses studio voice, class voice, classroom pedagogy and music education in the public schools.

Sarah Johnson has been invited to lecture to numerous musical organizations and institutions. Her paper, Group Instruction: An Alternative for the Freshman Voice Student, was presented in 1977 at the annual meeting of the National Association of Schools of Music, Chicago, Illinois. This paper was ultimately published in the National Association of Teachers of Singing Bulletin, March/April, 1979, Chicago.

TABLE OF CONTENTS

		Page #
Introduction		**vi**
Chapter 1	**REALIZING THE POTENTIAL OF YOUNG SINGERS**	**1**
	The Need for Voice Training in the High Schools	1
	The Voice Class Advantage	2
	Designing the Voice Class	3
	Units of Study for the Voice Class	5
	Unit 1-Guides to Effective Learning	5
	Unit 2-Breathing in Singing	8
	Unit 3-Resonance	17
	Unit 4-Phonation and Registration	21
	Unit 5-Articulation and Diction	25
	Unit 6-The Healthy Voice	34
	Unit 7-The Performance	37
	Teacher Guidelines	40
	Sample Lesson Plans	42
	Vocalises	46
	Vocal Repertoire for the Young Singer	49
	Summary	51
	References	51
Chapter 2	**CHORAL TECHNIQUES**	**58**
	Communication with Singers	59
	The Role of the Conductor	59
	Meeting the Singers: Interviews	60
	Auditions/Selection	61
	Seating	64
	Vocalization	66
	Rehearsals	75
	Elements of a Good Rehearsal	77
	The Conductor's Ear	79
	Rehearsal Reminders	80
	Changing Voices	82
	Non-Musical Factors	87
	Planning and Assessment	88
	Summary	92
	References	92

Chapter 3   **SINGING IN MULTIPLE LANGUAGES**   **95**

The International Phonetic Alphabet   95
Italian: The Singer's Language   97
Liturgical Latin   105
Spanish   110
Hebrew   117
German   121
French   133
Summary   148
References   148

Chapter 4   **EAR TRAINING**   **152**

Unit 1-Tonality in Major Keys: Movable Do   153
Unit 2-The Major Scales and Keys   158
Unit 3-Developing Tonal Memory in Major Keys   160
Unit 4-Dictation and Sight-Singing in Tonal
      Exercises: Major Keys   168
Unit 5-Meter and Notation: The Measurement
      of Sound   170
Unit 6-Melodic Dictation and Sight-Singing:
      Major Keys   174
Unit 7-Developing Tonal Memory in minor keys   175
Unit 8-Writing the Minor Scales   179
Unit 9-Dictation in Tonal Exercises, Melodic
      Dictation and Sight-Singing: minor keys   182
Unit 10 -Chromaticism   183
Unit 11-Intervals and Triads   187
Summary   195
References   195

APPENDIX   **Chapter 4: Ear Training (Student Worksheets) 197**

Unit 2 - Proficiency List:Major Scales & Keys   198
Unit 4 - Tonal Studies in Major   203
Unit 5 - Proficiency List:Rhythmic Proportion & Meter   207
      Rhythmic Patterns
Unit 6 - Proficiency List:Diatonic Melodies - Major (Treble)   210
      Diatonic Melodies - Major (Bass)   212
Unit 8 - Proficiency List:minor scales & keys   214
Unit 9 - Proficiency List A: Tonal Studies in minor   221
      Proficiency List B: Diatonic Melodies: minor (Treble)   225
      Proficiency List C: Diatonic Melodies: minor(Bass)   227
Unit 10-Proficiency List: Diatonic Melodies Using Chromaticism   229
      Chromaticism in Major Scales
      Chromaticism in minor Scales

INTRODUCTION

This book was written to assist the conductor of choral music in the educational process of improving the choral sound, especially in the junior high/middle school and senior high school. Choral music, by its very nature, is an example of active learning. Singers must be involved in making music in order to learn, to improve, and to accomplish a satisfactory performance.

If there is a connecting thread throughout the book, it is based upon the triangular concept of musical experience that takes place in singing: Imagery - Science - Sensation. Perhaps this can be compared to learning through mental - physical - emotional means. The art of singing is certainly a combination of all three, each influencing the others.

Singing well in a group is a musical phenomenon calling for musical discipline and social team work among the singers. One of the joys of a successful season is the feeling on the part of both singers and conductor that something of significance has been accomplished and will be remembered as time well-spent together. The experiences of self-realization and closure have taken place, for both the conductor and the members of the ensemble. It is the purpose of this book to lead the conductor to that goal.

A highly practical approach has been taken in presenting various topics: how to work with the voice as a changing and growing musical instrument; how to develop a "characteristic" choral sound; how to organize rehearsal time and effort; how to utilize multiple languages in choral singing; and, how to develop a curriculum for training the voice and the musical "ear".

1. REALIZING THE POTENTIAL OF YOUNG SINGERS

With a voice of singing
Declare ye this and let it be heard.
Alleluia! (WITH A VOICE OF SINGING, Martin Shaw)

This is a book about singing and the joy of singing together. Skills that relate to inspiring our students to love music through the choral experience are our concern here, and so "the voice of singing" becomes our first consideration.

THE NEED FOR VOICE TRAINING IN THE HIGH SCHOOLS

Why should your high school offer vocal training? There are "natural singers" who, like "natural athletes" seem to possess vocal talent, vocal coordination and a good ear before any musical or vocal training is begun. They are rare! Much more common is the student with an interest in music and an acceptable voice, but little knowledge, learned or instinctive, of how to sing. Both of these kinds of students will benefit from instruction in voice production. The 'natural' will gain understanding of the process and develop his/her talents more quickly. This knowledge and systematic training will guard against formation of poor habits which might later lead into vocal problems. The average singer will quickly find that he/she can become a much better singer than was expected. As correct vocal technique is learned and practiced, a new and better sound will emerge, instilling confidence and enthusiasm.

The benefits of some type of instruction in vocal production within a high school music curriculum are obvious. As individual voices improve, the choral program potential expands. Vocal blend and tone quality are perhaps the most obvious gains. In addition, vocal range, flexibility and dynamic control will improve and provide the director with the potential to explore more advanced and rewarding literature. Singing is an athletic pursuit and as endurance and vocal technique improve, vocal health will also improve, providing the director with a healthier, more dependable group of singers. And finally, the self-confidence of the individual singers will grow, encouraging them to try new situations and explore new areas of potential growth, both in music and in other areas of their lives. Self-esteem in teenagers is a commonly discussed subject in these days of drug and alcohol addiction as well as other social problems in our schools. Music and the self-confidence gained through successful performance can help the personal growth and self-esteem of our students.

THE VOICE CLASS ADVANTAGE

Should you try a voice class? Hopefully you agree that instruction in vocal production would be a positive addition to a high school music program. But let's be realistic. There aren't enough hours in the day to see all those students individually. The voice class can be your solution. Whether taught by you as choral director or by an area voice teacher in whom you have confidence, such a class can not only overcome time strictures, but also can be the most effective method of beginning voice study. In the field of voice instruction, certain singing skills can be taught more effectively to a group of students than to individual students and with fewer teaching hours invested. The following instructional goals and their implementation emphasize the advantages of this group approach.

1. *The formation of a basic singing technique.*
As students are guided in the learning of proper breathing patterns, relaxed articulation and efficient resonation, they not only hear instructions given to them individually, but they also monitor the same information being given to other members of the group. They are able to hear and see changes in their classmates. This results in reinforcement of their own subjective experience.

2. *Understanding of vocal production.*
The class format permits discussion of the components of vocal production. As students study together and then observe each other singing, they are given graphic examples of the function of the vocal instrument. Differing voice types and a variety of vocal problems expand their understanding of vocal production and potential.

3. *Growth in musicianship and interpretation.*
Students quickly learn to spot musical inaccuracies in each other's performances. Indeed, peer evaluation at this point is a very useful tool in challenging musical excellence. The immediate feedback of audience reaction on a regular basis very quickly helps a student realize the strengths and inadequacies of his/her interpretative ideas. Discussions of motivation, poetic intent, and communication greatly increase the growth in this area. The larger amount of literature covered is another growth factor.

4. *The development of self-confidence in performance.*
The regular opportunity to perform before others obviously helps develop self-confidence. Once again, group analysis of what constitutes an effective performance and experimentation with various aspects of stage deportment help to strengthen the student's self-concept. It is

interesting to watch the voice group serve as a support system for each member as they progress to other singing activities.

It is our experience that this approach to beginning voice instruction is not only a more efficient use of time but also a much more satisfying methodology to the teacher than the repetition of the same basic message individually to beginning students. Even more important, we are convinced that vocal progress moves more quickly and vocal technique is more thoroughly learned in the voice class.

DESIGNING THE VOICE CLASS

How should a voice class be structured? A voice class is most efficient with a group of 6 to 10 students. The mixing of various voice classifications enhances the learning experience. Ideally, two class periods of 50 minutes each should be scheduled weekly, however, one weekly class can be effective. A well ventilated room with good lighting and large enough to allow for some movement activities is important. It should be equipped with a well-tuned piano, straight-backed chairs and at least one music stand. A full length mirror and a cassette recorder would be ideal, and access to video taping is also a great advantage.

It is important to remember that this is not a small chorus. Although vocalizing and relaxation and posture exercises will usually be done together, the emphasis will be placed on individual performances of the music studied. Sometimes everyone will study the same song, particularly early in the course, but the goal should be to move to a variety of songs, each suited to the individual student.

At the first class session, expectations for the class should be spelled out. In addition to your attendance policy, grading, etc., the following goals should be presented, and used as a guide to measure progress throughout the year.

VOICE CLASS GOALS

1. Good posture - an attractive, confident appearance which facilitates correct breathing and relaxed singing.

2. Controlled deep breathing - a comfortably expanded rib cage, motionless upper chest, quiet inhalation, controlled exhalation, keeping the rib cage expanded.

3. The ability to sing pure vowels and, when appropriate, to sing diphthongs so that the mouth remains open as long as possible, i.e., as long as the word remains intelligible.

4. The ability to pronounce consonants so that the lower jaw remains relaxed and the tongue is flexible, moving to a low position after each consonant is executed.

5. The ability to use the International Phonetic Alphabet (IPA) as an aid to correct pronunciation of English and other languages the director may wish to use.

6. Understanding of vocal resonance and how to 'tune in' the best frequencies in your voice.

7. Awareness of your own vocal abilities, range, dynamic capabilities and the general characteristics that identify your voice as uniquely you.

8. Understanding of how to practice efficiently and how to thoroughly study a song.

9. The ability to present a song before the class with poised stage presence.

10. Awareness of how the skills learned in this class should carry over into choral singing. Specifically, what skills will remain the same and which ones will be modified when singing in a group.

11. Understanding of how good health habits effect singing, and when it is appropriate to sing or just learn by listening when certain physical symptoms are present.

12. Finally, the overall improvement of your singing ability so that your enjoyment and appreciation of singing is increased.

Now that philosophical and logistical issues have been discussed and class goals have been set, it is time to turn our attention to the content of a high school voice class. The next section of this chapter addresses the student and will deal with the specific topics and materials to be taught in such a class.

UNITS OF STUDY FOR THE VOICE CLASS

UNIT 1
GUIDES TO EFFECTIVE LEARNING

As you, the student, now begin your voice study, some specific guidelines will help you to learn efficiently and thereby develop your voice so that you will sing with a pleasant sound that can be enjoyed by you and others, and at the same time learn more about how your voice is produced. In addition, your musicianship will improve as will other skills that will help you become a good choral singer.

The Practice Session

A well planned, regular practice session is necessary if you are to learn efficiently, develop increasing vocal stamina and maintain a healthy voice. Unlike the instrumentalist, the vocalist who damages his/her voice cannot go out and buy a new instrument, for the voice is the instrument! Therefore, daily, intelligent practice time which develops good habits and a healthy voice is very important.

To help you plan a definite daily practice procedure, be sure you write down any instructions given by your teacher. Do not rely on your memory! Be sure to ask questions about any instructions you don't understand and have your teacher demonstrate any exercises that are unclear. A good practice session could include the following;

1. Stretching and relaxation exercises to help prepare you to sing.

2. Breathing exercises.

3. Vocalizing with vocalises assigned by your teacher for vocal development and stamina as well as those given to correct specific problems. Think about the purpose of each vocalise as you practice it.

4. At frequent intervals check your posture and facial expression in the mirror (a very important part of your practice equipment).

5. Now turn to the songs you are studying and follow the procedures outlined in the next section of this unit.

6. Do not become overly dependent on the piano as you practice. You need to give your full attention to the vocal technic you are developing.

The length of time you practice is governed by many outside factors, but the following considerations are important:

1. When you are a beginning student several short sessions will be more effective than one long session.

2. Once your voice begins to tire, vocal technic will deteriorate quickly. To increase your endurance, practice just a few minutes past the onset of fatigue, then stop and give your voice a good rest.

How to Study a Song

When learning a new piece of music the most common approach is to sing the song over and over without much thought being given to its components. This is not only inefficient but also leads to the repetition of mistakes which then become firmly planted in the memory. Breaking down the learning task into several parts will lead to more thorough knowledge of the piece and a learning pattern that helps good singing technic rather than getting in its way. Following is a suggested approach for learning a song:

1. As you first look at the song, note its structure and form paying particular attention to repetition of melodic and rhythmic passages and the relationship of the accompaniment to the vocal line. Also note the structure of the poetry, the rhyming words and repeated phrases.

2. Clap through the piece rhythmically. Isolate difficult sections, mark them and work them out thoroughly before continuing.

3. Play the melodic line on the piano and note difficult intervals. Mark them and analyze their relationship to the accompaniment. Establish a mental concept of the melody.

4. Read the text out loud, note the rhythmic flow and words which will benefit from coloration. Consider the text and music as a whole and mark temporary breathing patterns.

5. Using syllables such as <u>ta, mi, le,</u> which will facilitate easy vocal production and good placement, sing through the song until it is comfortably familiar. Notice this is the first point at which the singing voice is used.

6. Add the text, revising breathing marks if necessary. Mark initial and final consonants which need special attention. Indicate where diphthongs are found and note how they will be sung.

7. In subsequent practice sessions, review the steps above as they are needed. Eventually, No.6 will receive all your attention.

8. If this song is to be memorized the next section will help you.

Memorization of a Song

Ease of memorization is founded on systematic learning. If you have taken the time to analyze the components of your music as outlined in the last section, memorization will be well under way. The final steps to memorization are as follows.

1. Turning again to form, note the musical and textual phrases that are repeated. Pay particular attention to repetitions that are similar but not identical.

2. Be thoroughly familiar with the sound of the accompaniment to your song, paying particular attention to the introduction, interludes and postlude.

3. Study the text, no matter what the language and understand its meaning. Know the motivation and emotions involved in the words and you'll have reason to remember them. Writing out the text also helps to impress it on your memory. When words are consistently forgotten try this procedure, using the following phrase to illustrate.

"Be wary then and silent."

Presuming the word forgotten is "wary", begin by writing that word several times. Next, add the words preceding and following "wary". Finally write the whole phrase.

Example: wary wary wary
be wary then, be wary then, be wary then
be wary then and silent, be wary then and silent

This is particularly effective if the word you are forgetting is the first word of a sentence. Note the following example.

"Wilt Thou thy heart surrender? __Then__ *give it cheerfully."*

Example: then, then, then,
surrender? then give,   surrender? then
give
heart surrender? then give it.

4. Colorful marking of either the music or the text often help to imprint troublesome passages as far as memorization is concerned.

5. The greatest aid to memorization is thorough understanding of the text. If you truly try to communicate a story or emotion to the listener, your involvement in this act will help to erase memory lapses.

UNIT 2
BREATHING IN SINGING

The flow of air from the lungs through the vocal cords of a singer is like the flow of gasoline from the tank to the engine of a car. Anything that inhibits the flow of that fuel along the way, will prevent the best performance of the engine, or, in the case of the singer, prevent the vocal cords from producing their best sound.

If you've ever observed a baby crying very hard, you've seen the area right below the rib cage be sucked in as he/she runs out of breath. As the baby stops crying just long enough to inhale, this same area balloons outward as the lungs have filled with air. This is exactly the action that a singer must develop to sing with good breath control.

In addition to the physical action just described, the singer learns to control the rate of exhalation. Unfortunately, as that baby grows older, he/she may develop the habit of lifting and tensing the shoulders and upper body upon inhalation. When this happens, the area below the rib cage seems to be sucked in, the exact opposite action from what is necessary for the deep relaxed breathing needed for singing.

Some students naturally use deep controlled breathing when they sing, others will have to learn this skill. It is important for either group to understand this process, for even the student with a good natural breathing technique may acquire bad breathing habits in the future because of fatigue, the demands of advanced literature or excessive tension. Awareness of the proper function of the breathing mechanism will help to prevent these difficulties. Incidentally, not only singers, but any woodwind or brass players will also need good breathing habits. Earlier in this section we spoke of the need to control exhalation, indeed, slow it down, when we are singing. During sedentary exhalation for every day tasks we may inhale as often as sixteen to eighteen times a minute. During singing, the inhalation rate will diminish to five to ten times a minute. Because of the length of musical phrases an increase in the lung space is used, the number of inhalations is reduced and the rate of exhalation is controlled.

As we begin the study of deep, controlled breathing for singing we'll need to be familiar with the following terminology.

Breathing Terminology

1. Diaphragm - the large dome shaped muscle that separates the torso into two main parts. (Diagram 1, p.54)

2. Thorax - the upper part of the torso: the chest, which contains the lungs and heart.

3. Abdomen - the part of the torso between the diaphragm and pelvis which contains the stomach, liver, and remaining viscera.

4. Rib cage - the system of twelve paired bones which encase the contents of the thorax.

5. Viscera - the internal organs of the body contained in the torso.

6. Intercostal muscles - the muscles controlling rib expansion.

7. Epigastrium:
    a. The upper part of the abdominal wall, over the stomach.
    b. The expanse felt below the arch of the ribs, above the waistline, often erroneously called the diaphragm

8. Abdominal Muscles - the 4 pairs of muscles which control the rate of exhalation

9. Diaphragmatic breathing:
    a. Inhaling by expanding the rib cage so the diaphragm descends. (Diagram 2, p.55)

b. Exhaling by steady contraction of abdominal muscles in opposition to the resistance of the diaphragm, keeping the rib cage expanded. (Diagram 3, p.56)

c. Synonyms - high abdominal breathing, intercostal-abdominal breathing, deep breathing.

9. Clavicular breathing - inhalation which raises the shoulders and upper chest and shows little or no expansion around the lower ribs and epigastrium. It affords little control of exhalation and may cause neck and throat tensions and is an undesirable form of breathing for singing.

The Singer's Posture

The posture that is described here establishes the most favorable conditions for voice production and efficient breathing. It also presents a confident and attractive appearance. Begin by placing the feet comfortably apart with one foot slightly ahead of the other. You should feel that your weight is well balanced over the balls of your feet, giving you a feeling of buoyancy. The correct body position is described well by William Vennard in Singing, the Mechanism and Technique:

"The head, chest, and pelvis should be supported by the spine in such a way that they align themselves one under the other - head erect, chest high, pelvis tipped so that the 'tail' is tucked in". (VENNARD, pg. 19)

If this posture is maintained, the pelvic bones support the viscera, the resonators (spaces in the mouth and throat which amplify the voice), are directly above the vocal cords and the rib cage is lifted and expanded. In addition, the shoulders are not lifted or pulled back, but remain relaxed as does the neck so that the head can turn freely. The lower jaw should neither jut forward nor be pulled back into the throat. This posture should eliminate tension of the shoulders, neck or jaw which will quickly interfere with efficient vocal production.

The Expanded Rib Cage

The diaphragm, that dome shaped muscle right below the lungs, must descend and flatten if the lungs are to inflate to their full capacity. This is impossible in a slouched position. To illustrate this, hold your hand in a cupped position, with the palm toward the floor. Flatten your hand, noticing the change in its circumference. Imagine that the cupped hand represents the diaphragm and is completely encased by a rigid, immovable structure, the slouched rib cage. As you can see, it would be impossible to flatten or lower the diaphragm. When the rib cage is lifted it expands and the lowering of the diaphragm becomes possible. Therefore, good posture begins to expand the rib cage.

To learn to expand the rib cage, try the following. Raise your elbows to shoulder height at your sides, in the manner of wings. Feel the lift and expansion of the ribs as you hold this position. Now lower your arms to a normal position, but maintain the same rib position. Notice that when this is done correctly, the shoulders are relaxed, supported by the rib cage. The expanded rib cage should be maintained through a whole song. Any time this expansion collapses the next inhalation will not be efficient or complete unless the rib cage is again expanded, a time and energy consuming task in the middle of a song. This expanded position also supplies you with a reserve of air which should only be tapped rarely, on the longest, most difficult phrases. Expansion should be thought of as the forerunner to inhalation.

Inhalation

Inhalation built on efficient rib cage expansion does not require forceful drawing of air into the lungs. It is also the most quiet way to take a breath. When your rib cage is expanded and your mouth open, air will rush in to fill the additional space, thus balancing the air pressure inside and outside the body. As this happens the intercostal muscles between the ribs help with further expansion, and the epigastrium also moves out. Internally, the diaphragm descends to its full potential, compressing the abdominal viscera. (see diagram 2, p.55). Vennard warns:

"Most uninstructed singers, when asked to take a deep breath, raise the chest, which is good, but at the same time they pull in the abdomen so that it cannot move. This forces the organs of the belly up against the diaphragm and makes a really deep breath impossible." (VENNARD, pg. 29)

Exhalation

Exhalation is a reflex action to inhalation. If no attempt is made to control the rate of exhalation this action is accomplished quickly. The abdominal organs or viscera press up against the diaphragm which in turn expels the air in the lungs and the breathing cycle is complete (see diagram 3, p.56).

Breath control is the slowing down of the rate of exhalation and the economizing of the air supply. The object of this controlled exhalation is to expend only the amount of air necessary to keep the vocal cords vibrating consistently in order that they may emit a steady tone. This control is accomplished by two sets of antagonistic muscles, the diaphragm and intercostal muscles, and the abdominal muscles. It is necessary that the pressure exerted by the abdominal muscles pushing the viscera up against the diaphragm be resisted by the counter-balancing pressure of the diaphragm and intercostal muscles. This balanced pressure allows the proper amount of air to be expelled at the desired rate of speed. The sensation of breath support can now be explained as the steadying control the diaphragm exerts on the upward thrust of the abdominal muscles.

When the balance between these two antagonistic forces is upset, one of two things happens. If the abdominal force is too great the throat muscles try to perform the necessary slowing down action and the ensuing throat tension results in a pushed or forced tone. Fatigue and poor physical condition often result in this particular imbalance, and such tension is the root of many vocal problems. With insufficient abdominal pressure, tone quality becomes insipid, lethargic and uninteresting because the air stream is insufficient to vibrate the vocal folds steadily and carry the sound to the resonators or amplifying system. Our goal is to economize the expenditure of breath, avoiding the two extremes just described.

Breathing in a Song

One of the most common breathing faults of young singers is the unprepared, hurried breath between phrases of a song.

"Take time for a good breath before each musical phrase, just as a cornetist does before he plays. There is more time than you think if you do not hang too long on the final note of the last phrase. While you are a student there is no harm in prolonging the pause between phrases while you drink in a full breath. By the time you are ready to sing in public, the habit of breathing a full breath more swiftly and silently will have been formed." (WATER, pg. 165)

This quotation from an article The Most Rapid Way to Improve Your Voice is by the singer Crystal Water, and appeared many years ago in ETUDE magazine. It remains good advice today. The hurried, unprepared breath quickly leads to clavicular breathing. The heaving chest indicates inability to get enough oxygen, and since the urge to breathe is triggered by lack of oxygen, a vicious cycle is easily set up. It is interesting to note that this essentially chemical reaction of oxygen depletion is what upsets breathing in performance. Under tension, our body burns oxygen more rapidly and therefore the brain sets off the inhalation stimulus at shorter intervals. It, therefore, becomes even more important to breathe deeply when nervous.

Another special problem in breathing within a song is the occasional need to breathe very quickly. The secret here is to be mentally prepared to do so. In studying a song, note the places that allow little time for inhaling. If necessary, 'steal' time from the last note of the previous phrase. To help imprint this mentally, cross out the last note and rewrite it with an appropriate note value and a rest on which to breathe.

Example: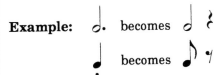

Remember, the key to quick inhalation is to expand quickly, not suck in air.

When no time is allowed for a full breath, singers learn to take a "breath on a breath". This means that after using only part of a normal breath supply, the singer keeps the unused portion under control and inhales a slight amount more. This technique is especially important in fast, florid singing.

Management of long phrases is always more difficult in the learning process than when the singer is familiar with the song. During this learning period the singer often teaches himself failure by continually running out of breath. Soon, trouble is anticipated at the end of the phrase. To prevent this stumbling block, learn a long phrase backward, (last two measures, then last four measures, etc.) thereby avoiding the memory of running out of breath.

To be prepared to breathe correctly for each phrase a singer must have a good concept of the phrase in its entirety - its length, expression, range and coloration. He/she must also have a good concept of his/her own best tone quality and a recognition of the part breathing plays in the total picture.

In summation, the singer should be able to inhale or exhale any volume of air up to maximum capacity, slowly or quickly. This then leads to singing with economy of breath. In the following section are a variety of exercises to use in developing each step of breathing as a singer.

Conditioning and Breathing Exercises

Physical Conditioning

For breathing to reach its highest efficiency, with the greatest amount of ease, the body must be in excellent physical condition. This requires a well balanced diet, plenty of sleep and appropriate physical exercise. Swimming, jogging, walking or any sport which requires controlled respiration will help strengthen the muscles used in deep breathing. Any exercise that improves your physical condition will improve your singing. It is unlikely that any other musical discipline is as quickly affected by fatigue and poor health.

The following exercises are particularly beneficial in conditioning the body for posture and breathing in singing.

1. Stretching exercises that emphasize the shoulders, neck, waist, chest and ribs
2. Sit ups
3. Leg lifts
4. Deep knee bends
5. Jumping jacks

Victor Fuchs, former German opera singer and teacher suggests the following exercises to strengthen the abdominal muscles. They are found in his book THE ART OF SINGING AND VOICE TECHNIQUE.

1. Stretch arms forward at eye level as for diving, swing them from one side to the other, spinning around from the waist without moving the feet.

2. Stretch the arms above the head and turn from right to left. When you turn right you lift the left arm and vice-versa.

3. Stand on tip-toe and bounce up and down in a quick rhythm, holding the arms sideways. (FUCHS, p. 82)

Vennard suggests the following exercise for posture, which he finds reminiscent of the statue "Winged Glory".

"A good exercise consists of swinging the arms circularly as if they were wings, rising on toes with each swing to add to the psychological effect." (VENNARD, pg.19)

Deep Breathing

These exercises are to be used at the beginning of a regular practice session to establish correct breathing habits. This collection of exercises is listed in the natural sequence of the components of deep breathing. Gradation of difficulty has been taken into consideration. Your teacher will help you choose those exercises most appropriate for you. Practice in front of a mirror for maximum benefit.

1. Expansion

a. Stand with shoulders against the wall, head also touching the wall, and breathe deeply. Once a position of expansion is obtained, there should be little movement of the upper chest or shoulders.

b. Notice the lack of shoulder action when you lay on a hard surface and breathe deeply.

c. Stand with your arms relaxed, your hand touching (not gripping) a chair by your side. As you inhale, notice if your hand moves upward on the chair. If it does you're raising your shoulders. Practice until you feel no upward movement by your hand.

Inhalation

Now that you have found a good, balanced posture for singing, practice the following exercises to develop good habits of inhalation. Observe yourself in a mirror.

1. To experience the correct feeling of the diaphragm-epigastrium movement, place one hand on the epigastrium, then try several of the following exercises, noting the action.

a. Say "O" as if surprised.
b. Yawn
c. Yell "hey" with good breath support.
d. Sing on a single pitch "ho, ho, ho".
e. Pant like a dog

At this point do not be concerned with the exact direction of the epigastrium movement, but only with getting these muscles to react.

2. Place one hand on the epigastrium and the other on the upper chest and inhale. Movement should be felt only by the lower hand.

3. Bend over, touch your toes and exhale. When you think exhalation is complete, blow out three more times. Now, without inhaling, stand erect with rib cage elevated. Place your hand on the epigastrium and do not inhale until absolutely necessary, then note the movement of your hand. Do not repeat too often or you may become dizzy.

4. Lie flat on the floor and place a sizeable book on the epigastrium. As you inhale, raise the book as far as possible. On exhalation, lower it as slowly as you can.

5. Place your hand over the side seams of your shirt and check for expansion of the sides of the rib cage as you inhale.

6. Place a pint size bottle or a similar object between your epigastrium and a wall. Stand in such a way that your body weight is leaning toward the wall. Release the breath without abdominal control. Let the bottle expel the air by pushing in below the ribs. Inhalation will push the body away from the wall. The amount of thrust will increase as diaphragmatic breathing is perfected. A clavicular (high chest) breather will have little or no thrust. (VENNARD, P.29)

7. Practice breathing on three counts, preparing mentally and checking expansion on the first count, inhaling on the second, exhaling on the third.

8. Next, to the count of four, prepare and inhale on 1, exhale over counts 2, 3, and 4.

9. If your breath is noisy, concentrate on expanding above the waistline so the air container is larger and the air rushes in. Do not suck air in. Be sure your mouth is open sufficiently.

Exhalation

While practicing these exercises, be sure the rib cage does not collapse as you exhale. Most of the conscious control will be with the abdominal muscles. Use the minimum amount of breath necessary for a good steady tone, but always use enough to maintain an open throat.

1. Inhale and, through pursed lips, with teeth apart, sustain a hiss. Do not permit the sound to become uneven. Begin by sustaining the sound for ten seconds. Work up to thirty seconds.

2. Inhale correctly, then sing on a medium range pitch, counting from 1 to 10 at first, then later working up to a count of 50. Never completely exhaust the air supply so that the rib cage drops or the throat becomes tense.

3. When you are walking, establish the following pattern in step with your gait. Inhale on 5 counts or steps, hold your breath for 10 counts, exhale on 5 counts. Repeat indefinitely.

4. Inhale slowly and at the same time slowly lift your arms from your sides to a "cross" position and then up over your head. With arms raised at the highest position hold your breath for a count of 5, then coordinate the slow circular descent of the arms with exhalation.

5. Sing up and down octave scales giving each note equal value. Begin with one complete cycle and work up to at least four.

UNIT 3
RESONANCE

For a singer to sing with the best vocal quality and be able to project the voice so it can be heard well, the study of resonance is very important. For this somewhat complicated subject to be discussed we need to begin with a series of definitions. Once some basic terms are understood, then the characteristics of resonance can be discussed in terms of sound, sensation and production.

Terminology

Resonance -*"the intensification and enrichment of a musical tone by means of supplementary vibration."* (WEBSTER'S NEW WORLD DICTIONARY)

"In singing, the vibration of the vocal cords causes sympathetic vibrations in the cavities of the throat, mouth and nose. The vibratory action of the air in these cavities amplifies the vocal cord tone greatly and determines the quality of the tone by suppressing undesirable partials. The tone heard by the listener is the result of a processing of the original raw vocal cord tone. This process takes place so fast that the production of the sound by the cords and its resonation by the

cavities seem to the listener to be simultaneous. The carrying power of a tone is not determined by volume, but by the quality of its production and resonation." (GREENWELL - Resonance, p.1)

"The quality of the vocal tone will be a product of the original glottal sound (see p.22, 'Glottis') *minus those overtones which were discouraged by the resonance cavities, plus the augmentation of overtones that were encouraged..."* (VENNARD, p.83, paragraph 299)

Harmonic Series - A succession of sounds consisting of a fundamental note and a series of overtones produced in mathematical proportion above the fundamental.

Fundamental - The tone which generates a series of harmonics.

Overtones - *"Any frequency emitted by an acoustical instrument that is higher in frequency than the fundamental."* (WEBSTER)

Partials - Overtones.

Vocal Cords - The original vibrators in the vocal sound.

Phonation - The production of a vocal sound by the vibratory activity of the vocal cords.

Sympathetic Vibration - The secondary vibration produced by resonators of the same frequency as the tone produced by the vocal cords.

Tuneable resonators - Those resonators whose size and shape can be changed by the singer, namely the mouth and throat.

Actuator - The initial source of power. In singing, the breath.

Bone Conduction - The transmitting of a vibratory sensation from the site of the resonating cavity to another area through connecting bone.

Formant - The resonator characteristics that produce a particular overtone frequency.

Resonance and the Harmonic Series

To illustrate how the harmonic series works, try the following experiment. After raising the lid of a piano, silently depress a key without allowing the key to sound, but allowing the string to vibrate freely. Next, sing the pitch of the key that is depressed. Stop singing and you will hear the tone continue as the piano string which was free to vibrate picked up the tone in sympathetic vibration. Now repeat the experiment but this time depress the sustaining pedal. Note the increased volume and the addition of other strings vibrating, showing the overtones that are sounding over the fundamental tone you have sung.

Royal Stanton in his book, Steps to Singing for Voice Classes, comments that 'resonance looks like re-sound' and that indeed describes what occurs when the fundamental tone produced by the vocal cords is picked up through secondary vibration in the throat, mouth and nose, which are acting as resonators and activating overtones that enhance and amplify the basic vocal sound. (STANTON, P.59)

How is Vocal Resonance Produced?

A resonant tone has a free unencumbered sound with clarity, warmth and richness. It will project so that it is easily heard by others. It feels free of strain and gives a sensation of tonal control. Through bone conduction it produces feelings of forward placement, sometimes referred to as 'singing in the mask'.

When the throat and mouth are relaxed it is possible to tune these resonators to produce the optimum resonance for any given vocal pitch and thereby enhance the vocal quality, amplify it and give the voice color appropriate for a given text. In order to get sympathetic resonation on every note, the resonators are constantly changed or tuned so their frequency of pitch matches that of the tone produced by the vocal folds. The frequency change is brought about by altering the size and shape of the throat and mouth and controlling the size of the opening into the nose. The amount of tension or rigidity of the jaw will also affect the tone quality. The mouth cavity changes shape and size by movements of the tongue, lips, jaw and soft palate. The throat size is altered mainly by forward flattening of the tongue and relaxation of the throat muscles. The position of the larynx also affects the size of the throat.

Once the mouth is opened adequately, adjustment of the resonators is essentially an internal process. Some of the earliest voice teachers would instruct their students to sing with an 'alive' expression aided by slightly raised cheeks. They also emphasized that the upper teeth should show slightly and the lower jaw should not be jutted out. Many teachers today would agree with these instructions. It is important to note, however, that excessive facial manipulation is distracting to the audience and should be avoided.

The trained ear of the teacher is the best guide to finding the most suitable formant for every pitch. This will vary with each vowel sound. Eventually the student should be able to hear and experience the proper formants. Vocalises designed specifically for tuning the resonance system will be found later in this chapter. In general, forward resonance is experienced when you sing or speak through a yawn. Exercises which make use of the beginning consonants *m, n, v, z* and the final *'ng'* sound are effective in producing desirable resonance which can be identified by the student.

Relaxation

Resonance is dependent on relaxation of muscles involved in vocal production. Excessive use of throat and mouth muscles will interfere with this process. Indeed, constriction is the beginning singer's most common fault.

When the student is unaware of excessive muscular tension in the lower jaw, lips, tongue, neck or shoulders, the following procedure may be helpful:

1. Tighten the fist and arm muscles with as much tension as possible.

2. Hold the arm and hand tense for ten seconds, then let go and note the sensation of complete relaxation.

3. Repeat this exercise tensing the muscles of the neck, back of shoulders, front of shoulders, tongue, lips and jaw individually.

It is important to learn to separate the actions of different muscle groups such as the tongue, the jaw, and those used for breathing. This is so the functions of one set of muscles do not increase tensions in the other muscular groups. The tongue must be trained to go to a neutral low position, touching the back of the bottom teeth when not being used for articulation. A relaxed jaw position can be learned by leaving space between the molars near the hinge of the jaw. Use YA, YA, YA, on a descending scale to be sure there is no setting of the throat or jaw. To separate jaw, tongue and breathing functions, alternate singing on YA, YA, LA, LA, HA, HA.

Daily Practice Suggestions

Set aside part of each practice session for concentration on resonance. Begin with exercises to relax the muscles involved with tuning resonators. Next, use vocalises assigned to promote resonance. Listen carefully to each pitch and 'tune it' accurately. Use a mirror to catch any excessive facial adjustments. When practicing a song, use some of the syllables that encourage resonance to warm up the voice before adding the words. Also use these syllables to work out vocally difficult phrases. Become aware of the sounds and sensations of resonant singing.

UNIT 4
PHONATION AND REGISTRATION

In the book <u>You the Singer,</u> Barbara Harlow calls the singer's voice an extraordinary gift which we develop into our own personalized musical instrument and which we then use as a transmitter of an idea conceived by a composer. (HARLOW, p.1) The very beginning source of this 'extraordinary gift' is the process which we will be discussing in this unit. But first, you'll need to know some basic vocabulary.

Terminology

Phonation - The production of a vocal sound by the vibratory activity of the vocal folds.

Vocal folds - sometimes called cords or lips, they are pearly white in color, covered by a thin mucous membrane. The folds lie horizontally in the larynx, parallel to each other, attached in the front. They open to a 'v' shape. Though their size will vary with the individual, they are approximately one-sixteenth to one-eighth inch wide, three-quarters of an inch long in men and one-half inch long in women.

Voice - Phonation plus resonance.

Vibration - The regular rise and fall in the pitch of vocal sound.

Pharynx - The cavity between the mouth and the larynx.

Trachea - The windpipe.

Larynx - The structure which encases the vocal folds. It is made of cartilage.

Epiglottis - The leaf-shaped cartilage forming a lid for the larynx. It keeps food from entering the lungs and permits the building up of air pressure within the body.

Glottis - The space between the open vocal folds.

Hyoid Bone - The u shaped bone at the base of the tongue from which the larynx hangs.

Velum - the soft palate.

Uvula - The soft, round protuberance hanging from the middle of the velum.

Register - An adjustment of the larynx which produces tones of a particular quality, for specific demands of range and dynamics.

Passagio - An area of register transition.

Timbre - The characteristic quality of a sound.

How Does Phonation Occur?

The process of phonation begins when air ascends from the lungs and sets the vocal folds in motion as it passes through the larynx. Because of the elasticity of these folds, they quickly move back toward a closed position. As this action is repeated in a fast rhythmical pattern, the vibration established produces a sound. The vocal folds are amazingly versatile, having the ability to vibrate their full length or only part of their length, and also to become thicker or thinner. The tension of the folds and the speed of their vibration can also change. These various characteristics of the folds determine the pitch of the tone sounded, its volume and timbre.

The initiating of a vocal sound is seldom a problem when the sound begins with a consonant. The task of coordinating the phonation for a sound beginning with a vowel can be more complex. If the vocal folds do not begin to vibrate just as the breath reaches them, the sound may be too breathy or may have a hard, plosive sound. This latter condition is called a glottal attack and can be very hard on the vocal folds, as it causes them to come together with considerable force which can in time cause a callus-like irritation referred to as a node. This is a very serious problem, therefore the beginning singer should avoid glottal attacks. There are times when experienced singers will use this attack, particularly in singing German. They learn to do it in a way that will not be detrimental to their voices. Exercises to develop smooth, coordinated vocal attacks will be found at the end of this chapter.

Sometimes singers get in the habit of stopping a tone, in other words, halting the vibration of the vocal folds, by tensing the throat. This is unnecessary and counter-productive. To stop a vocal sound, all one need do is inhale.

Vocal Registers

A logical question to consider at this time is how such tiny vocal folds can produce such a wide range of sounds. If you look at the strings of a piano that produce sounds in a given range of 2 to 3 octaves you'll notice that there is a large difference in the length of the highest and lowest notes you are considering. Indeed, there is a gradation of string lengths from the shorter strings producing the high notes to the long strings producing the low notes. If you look closely you'll also see that the piano strings are very thin for high notes, but become thicker for lower pitches, eventually being wrapped with copper wire to increase their thickness.

Now let us go back and consider the human vocal folds, less than an inch long and yet able to produce 2 to 3 octaves of sound. How is this possible? As a singer sings through all the notes in his/her range, the vocal folds go through certain adjustments in order to vibrate the correct frequency for each note. These adjustments alter the length and thickness of the folds and the speed of their vibration. Although some of this alteration takes place for each pitch, there are major changes that occur in all voices that are known as register changes.

You have observed the difference in riding with an inexperienced driver in a car with standard gear shift, and an experienced driver in a car with automatic transmission. With the first driver you are very aware of each time the shifting of gears occurs. The ride is bumpy and uncoordinated. With the second driver the ride is so smooth it seems as if no gear shifting occurs. The singer may start out with a problem moving smoothly from one vocal register to another, like the first driver. With training, the same singer will learn to blend these register adjustments so that 'gear-shifting' is replaced by 'automatic transmission' and the voice produces one smooth, coordinated, even scale throughout its full range.

There are two major adjustments of vocal folds which account for the light register and heavy register sound productions. The light register is produced with thinned folds which are under light tension. The heavy register requires thicker folds with more contraction of the muscles controlling their action. The higher range of the voice is produced by the light register, and likewise, the lower range requires the heavy register if it is to be produced with any volume. The middle area of the voice, sometimes referred to as the mixed register, combines the high and low register coordination. A good analogy would be the mixing of paint. If we start with a bucket of white paint and slowly add increasing amounts of red paint, we will see many different shades of pink as the mixture gradually darkens. Thus it is if we start with vocal sound which is produced with only the light register. In the range where the registers overlap the voice will change timbre as the lower register gradually is added, until finally the lower sounds are produced with only the heavy register.

If the adjustments between registers are not made smoothly there can be a very abrupt change of sound sometimes called a break. In the book <u>Fundamentals of Singing for the Voice Class.</u> Charles Lindsley describes this occurrence as follows:

"The reason the register break occurs.....is that in the lower register the vocalis muscles contract increasingly with ascending pitch until they can tense no more - the break releases the tension." (LINDSLEY, p.55)

Harlow describes this phenomenon of forcing the heavy register up too high as "trying to ballet dance in ski boots." (HARLOW, p.11) Forcing the heavy register (sometimes called the chest voice) too high in the voice is a common problem for altos and bass-baritones. The solution is to teach them the use of the lighter register (sometimes called the head voice) and then teach them to blend the two registers. This is most successfully done by starting in the light register and descending into the heavy, gradually mixing the two. The descending scale prevents the accumulation of too much muscular tension while this skill is being learned. Sopranos and tenors will probably use the light register more predominantly in their voice production and may need to learn to use the heavy register.

Those areas where register shifts occur are called the 'passagio', literally, the passage. These passages are most easily navigated if the following procedures are followed.

1. Be sure the head and neck alignment allows for relaxing of any excessive tension in the muscles affecting phonation, particularly in the area of the jaw, tongue and hyoid bone.

2. Increase the amount of air flowing through the vocal cords.

3. Keep the larynx in a comfortable position, neither too high or too low.

4. Use frontal resonance as you sing through this area.

5. Do not force the adjustment but let it occur gradually, in a relaxed manner.

It is interesting to note that some singers possess a natural coordination of the vocal registers and need little training in this skill. Most singers, however, will need to learn how to make adjustments in the passagio areas. The exercises at the end of this chapter will develop this skill. Additional suggestions will be made in chapter II.

UNIT 5
ARTICULATION AND DICTION

Singers share with other musicians the joy of making music. The unique quality of their art is the ability, in most cases the necessity, of expressing themselves with words and music. This adds the task of mastering articulation and diction to the already complex set of skills we use as singers. We must communicate with an audience not only the intentions of the composer but also of the poet. What a challenge! The objective of this unit is to teach you how to most efficiently produce the sounds needed to combine music and words and then weave them together to communicate to the listener verbally and musically. This means singing words that are easily understood and that still allow you to produce your best singing quality. Its time to begin with some new terminology.

Terminology

Articulation -The adjustment of speech organs to shape vowels and consonants.

Enunciation - The adding of phonation to articulation.

Diction - The integration of vowels and consonants into words and phrases in a manner that can be easily understood by the listener.

Articulators - The lips, mouth cavity, tongue, velum, jaw, pharynx, larynx.

Alveolar ridge - The ridge behind the upper teeth.

Hard palate - The roof of the mouth.

Soft palate - The flexible extension of the hard palate, the velum.

Phonetic - Pertaining to speech sounds.

I.P.A. - The International Phonetic Alphabet, symbols representing each sound in a given language, regardless of its orthographic spelling.

Orthographic - The spelling of words and sounds as they exist in a given language.

Pure vowels - A simple vowel sound that does not migrate to another vowel sound.

Diphthongs - A sound in which one vowel migrates to another. Not necessarily written as two vowels.

Voiced consonants - Consonants with phonation.

Unvoiced consonants - Consonants without phonation.

Plosives - Consonant sounds produced by the compression and sudden release of breath.

Linking - Blending the final sound of a word with the beginning of the next.

Articulation of Vowels

If we are to learn how to sing intelligibly while maintaining a good vocal sound, we must first learn how verbal sounds are produced. Vowels are shaped by the pharyngeal cavity, in fact there is evidence that they are influenced at the laryngeal level. The sound of specific vowels is determined first by the thought process and then by the size and shape of the mouth and pharynx. The position of the velum and tongue will effect these cavities, the vowel that will be produced and the resonance that enhances the basic sound. The velum or soft palate can be raised or lowered, thereby sealing off the opening to the nose or opening that area. The feeling of a raised palate is experienced in the beginning of a yawn and also immediately following the articulation of k or g. The tongue can be raised, lowered, curled back or thrust forward, or the back of the tongue can be raised in a hump. In addition, excessive tension in the muscles controlling the tongue, jaw and throat can alter the vowel sound that is being produced.

Vowels unify tone and assist in resonance. They are more important to intelligibility than consonants because they are sustained longer. This is the main difference between vowels in speech and vowels in song. A vowel which is held is vulnerable to gradual alteration of the sound if the mouth alters its size or shape while the note is sustained. This movement is referred to as vowel migration, and will be discussed later in this chapter in relation to the singing of diphthongs.

It is sometimes necessary to purposefully modify a vowel sound to maintain the best vocal quality on a given note. This will be discussed later in the chapter.

Articulation of Consonants

Consonants are formed by altering the exhalation of the breath stream. The articulators used here are the lips, tongue, teeth, and soft palate. They form consonants by temporarily stopping the air flow (p, t), by narrowing the air flow (s, w), by raising the soft palate (ng, k). Articulators can work in different combinations to produce specific consonants. For example, the lips can form (m), or the lower lip and the upper teeth can form (v). The tongue and the teeth can articulate (t) or the tongue, by thrusting forward can articulate (j).

The International Phonetic Alphabet

As we continue in our discussion, relating articulation to easily understood singer's diction, it is appropriate to introduce the International Phonetic Alphabet, or IPA. This subject will be discussed in greater detail in chapter III, but a brief introduction to it at this time will facilitate the discussion of specific sounds. Below you will find a chart with two columns. The first column will show the IPA symbol for a specific sound. The second column will present a word with the letter(s) underlined which illustrate the appropriate sound.

IPA Symbols Illustrating Sounds Found in English

VOWELS

IPA Symbols	English Examples
ɑ	f<u>a</u>ther
a	c<u>a</u>t
e	h<u>a</u>te
ɛ	g<u>e</u>t
i	f<u>ee</u>t
ɪ	<u>i</u>t
o	g<u>oa</u>t
ɔ	<u>aw</u>ful
u	b<u>oo</u>t
ʊ	p<u>u</u>t
ə	th<u>e</u>

CONSONANTS - Many consonant IPA symbols are the same as the orthographic letter in English. This chart does not repeat those symbols but only lists those which will differ.

<u>IPA Symbols</u>	<u>English Examples</u>
ŋ	si<u>ng</u>
ɲ	can<u>y</u>on
ʎ	bri<u>ll</u>iant
j	<u>y</u>ou
θ	<u>th</u>ink
ð	<u>th</u>is
ʃ	<u>sh</u>e
ʒ	plea<u>s</u>ure
h w	<u>wh</u>en
ʧ	<u>ch</u>ew
t s	boa<u>ts</u>
ʤ	ju<u>dg</u>e
d z	a<u>dds</u>

Now that you have been introduced to the IPA symbols, they will be used to illustrate the sounds we will be discussing. *They will <u>always</u> appear in brackets unless clearly labeled in a chart.*

Vowels and Their Modification

Because vowels are the sounds that allow for the most resonant, open tone, singers learn to hold on to them as long as possible. This means that you must learn to think of syllables in singing differently than they would be found in a dictionary, or, for that matter, printed as a song text. Let's look at the word 'absolutely' as an example. It is most often broken into syllables as follows: ab-so-lute-ly. The singer would sing it as follows: a-bso-lu-tly. Notice that each syllable now ends with a vowel, prolonging that sound, and the singer moves to the consonant only when ready to move to the next syllable. As beginning singers it would be helpful for you to mark the text of any song you are singing in voice class or your choral ensemble so that all syllables end in vowels as has been illustrated The one exception will be the final syllable of a work, but even then the final consonant(s) should be delayed (co-nso-na-nt).

Within a phrase this idea is carried a step further in what we call linking. That is, the end of one word is pronounced with the beginning of another word to help the legato line and carry out the principle of singing on vowels as much as possible. Below is an example of a phrase as it would be written and then as it would be modified for singing.

Example: "When morning gilds the skies"
[h w ɛ - n m ɔ - n i - ŋ g ɪ - l d s ð ə - s k ɑ - ɪ z]

There are exceptions to this rule which follow. In her book The Singer's Manual of English Diction, Madeleine Marshall notes the following exceptions to the practice of linking:

"When a word ends with the same vowel <u>sound</u> that begins the next word.....
 Example: three / eagles

When a work of importance might be mistaken for another word.....
 Example: her / ear

When a word beginning with a vowel requires special emphasis for dramatic effect.....
 Example: my / endless misery" (Marshall, p.64-66)

A different kind of a problem occurs in words that end in 'le', such as battle. Because the sustaining of the sound l is unattractive, the neutral vowel sound (sometimes called a schwa), is inserted so that a vowel sound can be sustained. See the example below.

Example: little becomes [lɪ-təl]

Earlier in this unit we spoke of the problem of single vowels migrating and becoming diphthongs which may be inappropriate in singing. In English, we do this very frequently in speech and also in some styles of singing such as country-western. A diphthong is created when the mouth moves from one position to another while a vowel sound is sustained. This most often occurs as the mouth closes to form a consonant, or simply because of habit. The best vocal resonance is obtained when the mouth is left open as much as possible in singing. This means that the voice student must learn to reduce the time spent with the mouth narrowing or closing to form a consonant. Pure vowel sounds should be sung wherever possible, moving quickly to the next consonant so that no vowel migration is perceived.

Practice singing the Italian word se, [se] on an arpeggio, making sure that you keep the vowel pure, with no migration. Stop the sound before you let your tongue or jaw make any movement. Remember the feeling of this pure vowel. Now speak the English word, 'say'. In speech the two vowels forming the diphthong flow without interruption, giving no particular sense of closure. Now sing the word 'say'. Do you feel a tendency to go quickly to the second vowel, to make a closure too soon for the best resonance? This word contains a legitimate diphthong, one that is written [seɪ]. When correctly sung, the first vowel of the diphthong will be held until just before the end of the note or notes to be sung. In addition, the second vowel is de-emphasized and the more open form of the vowel sung, [I] instead of [i].

Example: say becomes [se -ɪ].

The common diphthongs are listed below, showing the delay of the 2nd vowel and its open pronunciation.

ɑɪ	light	=	[lɑ-ɪt]
eɪ	may	=	[me-ɪ]
ɔɪ	voice	=	[vɔ-ɪs]
ɑu	how	=	[hɑ-u]
ou	go	=	[go-u]

The last vowel issue to be addressed is the appropriate modification of a vowel in singing. This occurs in three instances.

1. When the voice ascends in its extreme upper range and sometimes in its lowest range.

2. As volume is added to the tone above mezzo-forte.

3. Occasionally for the purpose of coloring the text.

The reason these modifications are made is to facilitate the best vocal sound, allowing for ease of production and the tuning of the proper resonation. In the instances listed above, vowels will modify to the more open form of the vowel. For example, 'sing' will modify from [si] to [sɪ]. Care should be taken that modification only be used where necessary to improve the vocal sound. Inappropriate use of this principle will lead to diction that is mushy and difficult to understand.

Pronouncing Consonants

In a recent article on diction, by Sandra Kungle, published in the June 1988 volume of <u>Journal of Research in Singing and Applied Vocal Pedagogy,</u> consonants are described as 'those events which function more as a gesture or quick movement than as a sustained event," (KUNGLE - <u>JOURNAL OF RESEARCH IN SINGING,</u> Vol. XI, No. 2, p.33). Consonants are formed by impeding the escape of the outgoing breath stream. This is accomplished by the lips, tongue, teeth, soft palate and jaw. Quickly executed consonants prevent distortion of vowel sounds.

Consonants are produced with or without phonation. Many voiced and unvoiced consonants can be paired. That is, the articulation of the two consonants is the same, the only difference in their sound being phonation in the voiced consonant and no phonation in the unvoiced consonant. Below you will find a listing of these pairs.

UNVOICED CONSONANTS	IPA	VOICED CONSONANTS	IPA
t	t	d	d
f	f	v	v
p	p	b	b
k	k	g	g
th (as in thin)	θ	th (as in this)	ð
s	s	z	z
sh	ʃ	z (as in azure)	ʒ
ch	ʧ	g (as in George)	ʤ

Good diction requires that there be no confusion between paired consonants. This is a common mistake and can lead to such disasters as singing 'let us bray' when the words should be 'let us pray'. Voiced consonants which end a word need special attention.

When correctly produced, consonants can help to project the tone and text of a song. However, consonants produced with too much tongue or lip pressure can cause constriction of the articulators and the throat. The worst offenders are *l, m, n, r, v, w, z* and *th*. A tight jaw will prevent the proper opening in both the mouth and the throat and inhibit resonation. A tight jaw is a symptom of a tight throat. Shallow vowels will result and words such as 'shall' will be pronounced 'shell'. Lips should be relaxed when articulating consonants made by the lips or lip and tongue or teeth.

In European languages the consonants *l, d, t* and *n* are pronounced differently than they are in American English. The American tends to articulate these sounds with the tongue and the hard palate whereas the European produces the same sounds with the tongue and the upper teeth. This European method is much better for the singer in any language. The execution of the consonant takes place much more quickly and thereby returns the mouth cavity to an open configuration which promotes efficient resonance and a pleasant tone. The American *l* in particular is frequently prolonged and becomes an unpleasant sound as well as producing tension.

Another consonant that can be a problem in singing English is *r*. Here again we can learn from the Europeans, who use a frontally produced *r* with the tongue touching the alveolar ridge. Madeline Marshall states that *r*'s are never sung before a consonant, seldom before a pause, and always before a vowel. When an *r* is not produced, care must be taken to replace it with a continuation of the vowel sound that preceded it. (MARSHALL, p.9).

Example: 'lord' becomes [lɔ-d]

When an *r* is sung it is important to treat it as the beginning of a syllable, not the end.

Example: 'carol' becomes [kɛ- rə-l]

Singing Rapid Texts

The singer is presented with a real challenge when singing a fast song with many words. For this to be done effectively the words should be accurately memorized. Correct tonal production including forward vowels and clear consonants not disturbed by unnecessary facial manipulation is important. Dynamic levels from piano to mezzo-forte are most realistic. Careful planning of breathing patterns is essential.

The following quotation from Madeline Marshall is concerned with proper accent or stress in a sung text. It is particularly helpful when singing rapidly, but is important in all singing.

"A helpful prescription against squareness in music might read like this: Syllables must be sung as part of a word. Words must be sung as part of a phrase. Unstressed syllables must be unstressed....."
(MARSHALL, p.154)

UNIT 6
THE HEALTHY VOICE

In his book, <u>Secrets of Singing,</u> William Ross says *"a good singing technique is the best vocal hygiene."* (ROSS - p.92) The singer who has diligently worked at perfecting a good tone quality, agility, dynamic control, controlled deep breathing and the ability to sing in all registers is well on the way to vocal health. Good vocal condition can only be maintained by regular practice sessions that emphasize these components of vocal technic.

The health of the voice is dependent on the health of the singer in general. A nutritious, well balanced diet, plenty of sleep and physical exercise are essential. Emotional outlets to help deal with stress are also important.

Avoiding Vocal Abuse

The every day use of the voice is often overlooked as a potential source of vocal problems. It is fairly obvious that shouting, screaming and yelling are hard on the voice, particularly when done without adequate breath support and in a high range. School athletic events are often the scene of excitement which stimulates such yelling at a time when throats are tight and constricted.

Most people are unaware of the fact that coughing and clearing the throat also are potentially damaging to the vocal cords. Coughing cannot always be avoided, but can be subdued by steam inhalation, warm liquids and medications as prescribed by a physician. Throat clearing is often a nervous habit that can be broken by awareness of the habit and substitution of swallowing for throat clearing.

Some singers abuse their voices by forcing an inappropriate sound, singing too loud, or singing out of range. When this is a frequent occurrence the singer comes to accept the throat irritation he/she feels as normal and does not recognize it as a warning signal that something is wrong. Strong voices can take this treatment longer than more delicate ones, but will still end up in vocal trouble. When hoarseness or loss of voice occurs this is an indication that the vocal cords are swollen and rest from speaking as well as singing is important. A tired voice is also a warning that you should take it easy vocally.

Know Your Abilities and Limitations

The student must know his/her own normal vocal quality if he/she is to spot vocal trouble when it occurs. It is also important to be aware of your own limitations of endurance, range, tessitura. The extremes of volume, softest and loudest singing with a healthy sound, should also be understood. In this Voice Class you will be carefully monitored and guided in the development of these areas. Quality is always more important than volume. Good resonance projects the voice so it need not be forced. Appropriate breath support will help prevent muscular tensions that lead to vocal problems. Your teacher will guide you in the selection of appropriate song literature. Musical styles such as hard rock are definitely detrimental to the voice. On the other hand, the student with a love of opera must realize that this is very advanced literature in most cases which should not be attempted by the beginning singer.

Illness and the Singer

When should you, the singer, continue singing in the presence of illness and when is it dangerous to your voice to do so? This can be a hard decision to make and one which will frequently require consulting with a doctor as well as your choral director or voice teacher. Here are some general guidelines.

If you have a sore throat, huskiness or laryngitis, avoid singing and talking. Do not chatter away about how sore your throat is, how you can't sing, etc. Rest your voice! Talking can jeopardize your voice as much as singing.

With colds and sinus infections in which there is no throat involvement, some important performances may be considered after consultation with your doctor and your choral director or voice teacher. If you are well enough to be in school, routine rehearsals and Voice Class should be attended even if singing is inappropriate.

In general, anytime illness is present singing should be held to a minimum. Fatigue and poor physical condition invite vocal problems. Vocal technique often slips under these conditions. Breath support is often insufficient and as a result the voice may become driven by tension in the throat, jaw, shoulders, etc. Allow sufficient time for recovery before launching into your full singing program. The recovery period can be a time when bad habits begin because of the conditions just described.

Vocal Problems

Persistent or recurring vocal problems should be taken up with your teacher and possibly a laryngologist. Hoarseness, diminishing endurance, and areas of the vocal range in which it suddenly becomes difficult to sing are symptoms that need expert medical attention when they persist at the end of an illness or occur because of problems in voice use.

Many vocal problems begin with the speaking voice. In addition to the situations described in the section on vocal abuse, the following conditions can cause problems. Breath support and resonance are as important in speaking as they are in singing. Too often this is overlooked in daily speech. Cheerleaders who attempt to project their voices without knowing these basic technics often find themselves in vocal difficulty. Because we speak so much of the time it is common to be unaware of these deficiencies. Another area of potential speech problems is the habit of speaking in an inappropriate range. We have the capability of speaking with a wide variety of pitches, indeed we are more interesting to listen to when we do! Problems occur when the general range of our speech is too high or to low.

Student Health Responsibilities in Choral Singing

You are responsible for monitoring your voice in a choral situation. Be aware of the diminished ability to hear yourself and do not over sing because of this. If certain passages of a song consistently make you uncomfortable vocally, tell the director. Practice good vocal technic and posture. When you should not sing because of health problems see how much you can learn at a rehearsal without using your voice. Ask yourself how well you'll be singing in forty years, for the care you give your voice today will determine how long and how well you will sing.

UNIT 7
THE PERFORMANCE

And now for the performance! Although the Voice Class experience has been made up of many performances before your classmates, the time has now come to prepare for a public performance. There is much more to think about than just singing. The singer relates more directly to an audience than any other musical performer. As a result, he/she is evaluated on non-musical skills as well as musical skills, all of which are part of the total vocal performance.

This unit will help you to maximize the joys of singing for others and minimize the frustrations that are caused by feeling unprepared to face an audience. Although the performance addressed here is specifically the solo singer and pianist, the basic concepts can be applied to the choral singer in performances as well.

Preparation

The most successful performances are built on complete mastery of the music you will sing. Review Unit 1 on learning a song and memorization. Think through the mood and purpose of the song many times and plan how you will interpret it. Work frequently with the accompanist so you are both comfortable with your combined parts and have developed a good sense of ensemble. Use a tape recorder to help you evaluate your practice sessions. With the help of your teacher eliminate any unusual mannerisms, peculiar facial expressions or nervous habits such as clearing your throat, tapping your fingers, etc. Be aware of unplanned movements that detract from the performance. If any gestures are to be used be sure they are carefully planned and really enhance the song. Use them sparingly. Plan what you will wear giving thought to what will make you look attractive and neat. Clothes that are too flamboyant steal audience attention from your singing.

Be aware that the actual performance may make some changes in your singing. The excitement of the moment may mean your breath endurance will shorten. Have alternate breathing patterns worked out in long phrases which can be used should this happen. Another possible reaction to excitement is the speeding up of tempos. Be prepared to resist this impulse. Have a clear understanding with your accompanist as to how you will handle a memory lapse or other emergencies should they occur. It is very important to rehearse in the room in which you will sing and become used to the acoustics, the piano and the other physical properties of the area. Be aware of the acoustical difference between an empty and an occupied room. Include all the components of a performance in your rehearsal; the entrance, the singing, acceptance of applause and the leaving of the stage when you are finished. It is a good idea to have several people attend your final rehearsal to give you the feel of singing to an audience. Your voice classmates could be helpful here.

And now the time for your performance is almost here! You are excited, perhaps nervous. Do not give in to the impulse to talk rapidly and increase your nervousness. Rest your voice. Save it for the

performance. Try to spend some time by yourself and clear your mind
of unimportant things so it will be fresh to concentrate on your song.
Do some simple stretching exercises, vocalize, practice deep breaths for
singing.

Entrance and Preparation

The first impression you make on an audience is very important. In the
solo vocal performance the singer enters the stage first, followed by the
accompanist. Enter purposefully, expecting to enjoy this experience.
Exhibit a friendly but dignified attitude toward the audience.
Acknowledge their applause with a smile and slight nod of the head.
Think of them as your friends, not your adversaries. If you are lucky
enough to be performing with a grand piano, stand in the curved area.
With an upright piano determine ahead of the performance an area
where you are easily seen and heard by the accompanist as well as the
audience.

Now that you are comfortably in place, wait a moment for the audience
to become quiet. Give the accompanist time to arrange the music on
the piano, adjust the stool, etc. Prepare yourself mentally and
physically for the song you are about to sing. Think about posture, the
piano introduction, the text and the interpretation. Take a couple of
deep breaths to help make the transition from everyday breathing to
singer's breathing, and also to help quiet any nervousness you may be
feeling. When both you and the pianist are ready, give a slight nod,
lift the head or use some other signal you have planned with your
performance partner to signal you are ready to begin.

The Song

The song begins for both performers with the first note of the
introduction. You should be actively involved with listening to the
piano, not adjusting your clothing, counting the number of people in the
audience or letting your mind wander in any other way. Your audience
will be able to tell if you are not involved with the music, and what's
more, if your mind is wandering you might miss your entrance. This
will also be true later in the song when there are piano interludes.

Once you have begun to sing, concentrate on creating a mood,
expressing an emotion or narrating a story - whichever is appropriate.
Nervousness will be less of a problem if you don't consider what the
audience thinks of you but rather think of yourself as the medium

through which the music is being expressed. Do not concentrate on vocal technique, but always have it in the back of your mind. On the other hand, don't become so lost in interpretation that you forget where you are in the music and text. Have an agreement made ahead of time with the pianist as to what he/she will do should you have a memory lapse. Remember, the song does not end until the last note is played on the piano. Do not break the mood until it is released. Enjoy the performance!

Indicate the conclusion of the song by bowing your head, moving your hands or showing some sign of relaxation. Acknowledge applause graciously, and indicate your appreciation of your accompanist by encouraging him/her to bow also. Leave the stage walking decisively, but not hurriedly.

Coda

As you look back on your first solo performance we hope you have enjoyed it and noted the special communication there can be between a singer and an audience. The folksinger Judy Collins sums this experience up very well.

"It's incredibly inspiring to connect with an audience, but that's not to forget there's a learning process that goes on which permits it to happen. A lot of the extreme pleasure and satisfaction that are possible in this kind of work is knowing how to do it. There are things you simply have to spend time to learn - how to play, how to sing, how to project, how to think of a phrase as more than a string of single words. The object of a craft is to make you unaware of it and to transcend the music."
(COLLINS - LIFE, p.40A -40B)

Teacher Guidelines

As you begin to plan for your high school voice class you will combine material from the various units of study, the collection of vocalises and the suggested song collections. To help you with this task, three sample lesson plans are provided. As you design your own plans the following suggestions may be helpful.

1. Organize each class to include review of the previous lesson, relaxation exercises, thoughtful vocalization, class and individual singing.

2. Begin with all students studying the same song, but quickly move to individual assignments. Decide to go with a specific music series so that all students may follow along in their own books.

3. Use student leadership when appropriate, i.e. leading relaxation exercises, vocalizing or similar activities.

4. Remember the importance of positive reinforcement for individual performers. A non-threatening environment is necessary if they are to sing their best and be willing to experiment with new sounds, posture and ideas.

5. When No.4 is successful, students will be able to respond better to corrective criticism. Within this atmosphere, students should be encouraged to comment on their observations of their own singing and the singing of other class members.

6. We are training singers to learn by the following observations of themselves and others:

   a. What they feel as singers.

   b. What they hear as they sing, as others sing, and as they listen to audio tapes of their own singing.

   c. What they see in the mirror, as others sing, and by studying video tapes of their own performances.

7. We use a variety of methodologies in our teaching, finding the best approach for each student. Building on the principle stated in No. 5, we guide the students' observations. We present accurate scientific information as to how voice is produced, but rely heavily on imagery to help find given sounds and singing sensations. When this imagery differs from what actually occurs physically, we are sure the student understands this difference.

8. Varying voice types, vocal problems and personality differences should not be viewed as problematic in the voice class. Rather this variety should enhance the learning experience.

9. The carry over and co-ordination of voice class with choral ensembles is only limited by the creativity of the teacher(s) involved.

SAMPLE LESSON PLANS

The following lesson plans assume a class of six to eight students of varying voice types. The class meets twice a week for 50 minutes.

LESSON 1

Introduction to Voice Class

OBJECTIVES
1. Establish rapport with the group and between students.
2. Begin a record of each student, written background and observations and an audio tape of vocal progress.
3. Explore resonance sensations.
4. Begin the study of the first assigned song.

MATERIALS
Piano; student copies of *THE ARNOLD BOOK OF OLD SONGS*; handouts (Questionnaire, Class Goals, Units of Study for the Voice Class).

ACTIVITIES
1. Distribute the Voice Class Questionnaire and have students complete it (10 minutes).

2. Have students discuss their past and present music experiences, why they are interested in voice class, what they expect to get from the class (15 minutes).

3. Explain your expectations of the students (10 minutes).
   a. Attendance and grading policies.
   b. Organization of the class.
   c. Distribute and discuss Voice Class Goals.

4. Sing (12 minutes).
   a. Teach vocalises 1, 2, and 3 by rote.
   b. Discuss resonance sensations.
   c. Teach <u>Drink to Me Only With Thine Eyes</u>, from *The Arnold Book of Old Songs*.
      1) First sing on [mi]. (use [mo] on the highest notes)
      2) Alternate [mi] and [mo] with a phrase of words.
      3) Sing complete verse with words.
      4) Discuss the form of the song.

ASSIGNMENT
1. Read <u>Unit 1</u>, pages 6 - 9.
2. Practice <u>Drink to Me Only With Thine Eyes</u> and assigned vocalises.
3. Prepare a previously learned song to be sung and taped in the next class.

VOICE CLASS QUESTIONNAIRE

Name_____   Phone_____

Address_____   Age_____

_____   Class_____

Musical Experience

Lessons
Instruments_____   Years Studied _____   Current ?_____
(Including
voice)   _____

_____   _____   _____

Ensembles
Instrumental _____   Years of Participation _____   Current ?_____

_____   _____   _____

Choral _____   Years of Participation _____   Current ?_____

_____   _____   _____

_____   _____   _____

What part do you sing in Ensembles?

Soprano _____   Alto _____   Tenor _____   Bass-Bar. _____

Foreign Languages Studied
Language_____   Years Studied _____   Current? _____

_____   _____   _____

What are your current activities or hobbies?
School   Other

_____

_____

_____

_____

What is your favorite class?

_____

Why do you want to study singing?

_____

_____

LESSON 20

Singing Beautifully and Intelligibly

OBJECTIVES

1. Reinforcement of previously learned material.
2. Familiarity with new terminology.
3. Review of good daily warm-up routine.
4. Experiencing and comparing positive and negative diction habits.

MATERIALS

Piano; music stand; mirror; student tape recorders

STUDENT PREPARATION

1. Read Unit 5 - Articulation and Diction
2. Prepare assigned song

ACTIVITIES

1. Review material covered in the last class session (5 min.)
2. Give a quiz on the terminology in Unit 5 (15 min.)
3. Have a student lead stretching exercises emphasizing the neck, shoulders, rib cage, tongue, and jaw (3 min.)
4. Sing the following vocalises (7 min.)
   - **a.** Resonance - No. 2
   - **b.** Breathing - No. 6
   - **c.** Smooth attack - No. 7
   - **d.** Register blending - No. 11
   - **e.** Flexibility - No. 18
5. Study the diction problems presented in the assigned song Over the Mountain from The Arnold Book of Old Songs (18 min.)
   - **a.** Have the class sing the song
   - **b.** Teacher illustrates the correct and incorrect production of the following sounds, and students repeat the illustrations, using their tape recorders for later study
     1) Shallow vowels - sing [stipɛst], not [stipɪst] for the word "steepest"
     2) Diphthongs - sing [ma-utɛns], not [mautɛns], delaying the second vowel in the word "mountains"
     3) Premature consonants that short change the vowel - sing -[ra-ks], not [raks] for the word "rocks"
     4) European, not American "l" - use only the tip of the tongue on the upper teeth to produce this sound; do not "paint" the hard palate with the tongue; practice on the word "love"
     5) Eliminate "r" before a consonant, replacing it with the continuation of the vowel sound that preceded it; sing [ovə], not [ovər] in the word "over"

ASSIGNMENT

1. Review the section on the IPA in Unit 5.
2. Study today's tape.
3. Prepare an assigned song to perform for class critique of diction

LESSON 28

Preparation for the Student Recital

OBJECTIVES
1. Analysis of the components of a performance
2. Practice of performance skills

MATERIALS
Piano; accompanist

STUDENT PREPARATION
1. Reading of Unit 7 - The Performance
2. Memorization of assigned song

ACTIVITIES
1. Review of material covered in the last class (10 minutes)
2. Discussion of Unit 7 (15 minutes)
3. Relaxation exercises and vocalizing (10 minutes)
4. Individual performances critiqued by the teacher
(6 - 8min/student) include the following
    a. Entrance with the accompanist
    b. Acceptance of applause
    c. Communication with accompanist to begin the song
    d. The song, sung expressively, with good vocal sound and words that can be understood
    e. Attentiveness to the music during interludes
    f. Completion of the song
    g. Acceptance of applause
    h. Acknowledgement of the accompanist.
    i. Exit with the accompanist

ASSIGNMENT
1. Design an evaluation sheet to be used in critiquing class members, using the Units of Study as a guide.
2. Continue preparation of song for class evaluation.

VOCALISES

The following vocalises are divided into specific areas of technique, although many of them will work on several areas of development. Once a student has been introduced to all vocalises, a typical practice session should include some exercises from each area. Generally, an exercise should begin in middle range, and then move up or down by half steps. It is best to warm up the upper range with descending scales through the upper passagio before going to upper range from middle range.

Review of Chapter II will provide additional vocalises and suggestions for their use. Although designed as choral warm-ups, many of these exercises can be appropriately used in the Voice Class.

Resonance

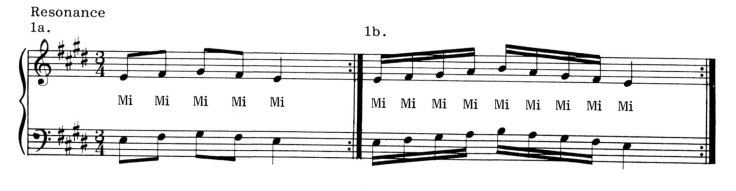

(for extension of breathing, complete full exercises up to 4 times)

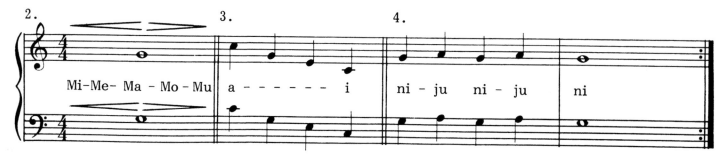

Breathing (see 1c & 2)

5.

a - - - n   o - - - - - - - - - -

6.

ha ha ha ha(etc.)

(also use hi, ho, he, hu)

7.

a _____

(also use
e, i, o, u)

8. (catch breath)

a _____   a _____   a _____

CHORAL MUSICIANSHIP

Register Blending (use no. 7 in transition areas)

Flexibility and Range

(boys begin with falsetto)

Vocal Repertoire For The Young Singer

Miscellaneous Collections of Song Literature

ALBUM OF NEGRO SPIRITUALS; Arr. H.T. Burleigh; C.P.P. Belwin, Inc.; High, Low; 12 songs; English

THE ARNOLD BOOK OF OLD SONGS; Arr. Roger Quilter; Boosey & Hawkes; Medium; 16 songs; English

ELIZABETHAN LOVE SONGS; Arr. Frederick Keel; Boosey & Hawkes; High, Low; 30 songs; English

EXPRESSIVE SINGING; Ed. Van A. Christy; Wm. C. Brown Company Publishers; High, Low
        Volume 1 (55 songs), Eng.,Fr.,Ger.,It.,Lat.
        Volume 2 (45 songs), Eng.,Fr.,Ger.,It.,Lat.

55 ART SONGS; Ed. Sigmund Spaeth and Carl O. Thompson; Summy - Birchard - Birch Tree Group Ltd.; Medium; Eng.,Fr.,Ger.,It.

OLD AMERICAN SONGS; Aaron Copland; Boosey & Hawkes; Medium; 1st set (5 songs); 2nd set (5 songs); English

OLD ENGLISH MELODIES; Arr. H. Lane Wilson; Boosey & Hawkes; Medium; 21 songs; English

PATHWAYS OF SONG; Ed. Frank LaForge and Will Earhart; M. Witmark & Sons; Warner Bros. Publishing, Inc.; High, Low
        Volume 1 (23 songs), Eng.,Fr.,Ger.,It.,Lat.
        Volume 2 (23 songs), Eng.,Fr.,Ger.,It.
        Volume 3 (24 songs), Czech.,Eng.,Fr.,Ger.,It.,Span.
        Volume 4 (26 songs), Eng.,Fr.,Ger.,It.

THE SONGS OF JOHN JACOB NILES; G. Schirmer; Hal Leonard Pub. Co. Dist.; Medium; 16 songs; English

STANDARD VOCAL REPERTOIRE; Ed. Richard D. Row; R.D.Row Music Co. Inc., Carl Fischer, Inc. Agents; High,Low;
        Book One (21 songs), Eng.,Fr.,Ger.,It.
        Book Two (22 songs), Eng.,Finn.,Fr.,Ger.,It.

24 ITALIAN SONGS AND ARIAS; G. Schirmer, Inc.; Hal Leonard Pub. Co. Dist.; High, Low; Accomp. tape available

28 ITALIAN SONGS AND ARIAS; Alfred Publishing Co. Inc.; High, Low; Accomp. tape available.

THE YOUNG SINGER; Ed. Richard D. Row; R.D. Row Music Inc., Carl Fischer Music Inc. Agents;

> Soprano (27 songs), Eng.,Fr.,Ger.
> Contralto (26 songs), Eng.,Ger.,It.
> Tenor (26 songs), Eng.,Ger.,Fr.
> Baritone (23 songs), Eng.,Ger.,It.

Songs From American Musical Theater

BROADWAY REPERTOIRE; Chappell & Co., Inc., Hal Leonard Pub. Co. Distributors.

> Soprano (15 songs)
> Mezzo-Soprano (15 songs)
> Tenor (15 songs)
> Baritone (15 songs)

THE SINGERS MUSICAL THEATRE ANTHOLOGY; Hal Leonard Pub. Co. Distributors.

> Soprano (46 songs)
> Mezzo-Soprano / Alto (40 songs)
> Tenor (42 songs)
> Baritone (37 songs)
> Duets (21 songs)

Supplemental Books of Vocalises

BUILDING THE VOICE AS AN INSTRUMENT; Vocalise Summary, p. 137; Pearl Shinn Wormhoudt; self-published

CONCONE - FIFTY LESSONS, OP. 9; G. Concone; G. Schirmer, Hal Leonard Pub. Co. Distributors.; High, Medium, Low

THE ESTELLE LIEBLING VOCAL COURSE; Ed. Bernard Whitefield; Chappell and Co. Inc., Hal Leonard Pub. Co. Distributors.

> Soprano
> Mezzo-soprano and contralto
> Tenor
> Baritone

MASTER VOCAL EXERCISES; Horation Connell; Theodore Presser Co.

Listings of Solo Vocal Literature

ART-SONG IN THE UNITED STATES, AN ANNOTATED
BIBLIOGRAPHY; Carman, Gaeddert, Myers, and Resch; A Publication of
The National Association of Teachers of Singing, 1976

MUSIC FOR THE VOICE; Sergius Kagen; Indiana Univ. Press., 1968

SOLO VOCAL REPERTOIRE FOR YOUNG SINGERS, ANNOTATED
BIBLIOGRAPHY; Ed. Joan Frey Boytim; A Publication of The National
Association of Teachers of Singing. 1980

SUMMARY

The purpose of this chapter has been to explore the various attributes of
singing: breathing, resonance, phonation, registration, articulation,
diction, and performance. In addition, we have tried to stress the need for
a healthy voice, guidelines for effective learning, and the advantages of
class voice instruction. Sample lesson plans, vocalises, a list of suggested
song literature, and a list of additional references have been included.

REFERENCES - CHAPTER 1

Collins, Judy; "I've Looked at Life from Both Sides Now", <u>LIFE</u>, May,
1969, p.40A-40B.

Fuchs, Viktor; <u>The Art of Singing and Vocal Technique</u>; John Calder;
London; 1963.

Greenwell, Gean and Jones, J. Loren; "What Happens in Singing";
Unpublished material prepared for voice class, Michigan State University,
1967.

Harlow, Barbara; <u>YOU, THE SINGER</u>; Hinshaw Music, Inc.; Chapel Hill,
NC; 1985.

Johnson, Sarah O.; "Group Instruction / An Alternative for Freshman Voice Students", THE NATS BULLETIN; Mar/Apr, 1979; p.20.

Johnson, Sarah O.; THE SOLO VOICE - A GROUP APPROACH TO SINGING; Wright State University; Dayton, OH; 1980.

Kungle, Sandra; "American English Diction - Idiomatic Pronunciation and Articulation Patterns and Some Implications for Vocalism, Intelligibility, and Projection"; JOURNAL OF RESEARCH IN SINGING AND APPLIED VOCAL PEDAGOGY, VOLUME XI, NO. 2; June, 1988; p.33.

Lindsley, Charles E.; FUNDAMENTALS OF SINGING FOR VOICE CLASSES; Wadsworth Pub. Co.; Belmont, CA; 1985.

Marshall, Madeleine; THE SINGER'S MANUAL OF ENGLISH DICTION; G. Schirmer, Inc.; New York; 1953.

Schøtz, Aksel; THE SINGER AND HIS ART; Harper and Row; New York; 1953.

Shaw, Martin; WITH A VOICE OF SINGING; G. Schirmer, Inc.; Hal Leonard Pub. Co. Dist.; New York; 1923.

Stanton, Royal; STEPS TO SINGING FOR VOICE CLASSES; Wadsworth Publishing Co.; Belmont, CA; 1983.

Vennard, William; SINGING, THE MECHANISM AND THE TECHNIQUE ; Carl Fischer, Inc.; New York; 1969.

Water, Crystal; "The Most Rapid Way To Improve Your Voice", ETUDE; Mar 1940; p.165.

Wormhoudt, Pearl Shinn; BUILDING THE VOICE AS AN INSTRUMENT; Published by author; Oskaloosa, IA; 1981.

SUGGESTED ADDITIONAL READINGS

Appleman, Ralph; THE SCIENCE OF VOCAL PEDAGOGY; Indiana Univ. Press; Bloomington, IN; 1967.

Coffin, Berton; THE SOUNDS OF SINGING; Scarecrow Press; Metuchen, NJ; 1976.

Kagen, Sergius; ON STUDYING SINGING; Dover Publications Inc.; New York; 1950.

Lessac, Arthur; THE USE AND TRAINING OF THE HUMAN VOICE; DBS Publications Inc.; New York; 1967.

Manen, Lucie; THE ART OF SINGING; Theodore Presser Co.; Bryn Mawr, PA; 1976.

Miller, Kenneth E.; PRINCIPLES OF SINGING; Prentice-Hall Inc.; Englewood Cliffs, NJ; 1983.

Miller, Richard; ENGLISH, FRENCH, GERMAN, AND ITALIAN TECHNIQUES OF SINGING; Scarecrow Press; Metuchen, NJ; 1977.

Reid, Cornelius L.; A DICTIONARY OF VOCAL TERMINOLOGY; Joseph Patelson Music House Ltd.; New York; 1983.

Ristad, Eloise; A SOPRANO ON HER HEAD; Real People Press; Moab, UT; 1982.

Ross, William E.; SECRETS OF SINGING; Published by author; Bloomington, IN; 1959.

Sable, Barbara Kinsey; THE VOCAL SOUND; Prentice-Hall, Englewood Cliffs, NJ; 1982.

Smolover, Raymond; THE VOCAL ESSENCE; Covenant Publications Inc.; Scarsdale, NY; 1971.

Sundberg, Johan; "Acoustics of the Singing Voice"; SCIENTIFIC AMERICAN; pp. 82-91, MAR, 1977.

Sundberg, Johan; THE SCIENCE OF THE SINGING VOICE; Northern Illinois Univ. Press; DeKalb, IL; 1987.

Uris, Dorothy; TO SING IN ENGLISH; Boosey & Hawkes; New York; 1971.

Winsel, Regnier; THE ANATOMY OF VOICE; Exposition Press; New York; 1978.

DIAGRAM 1 - DIAPHRAGM

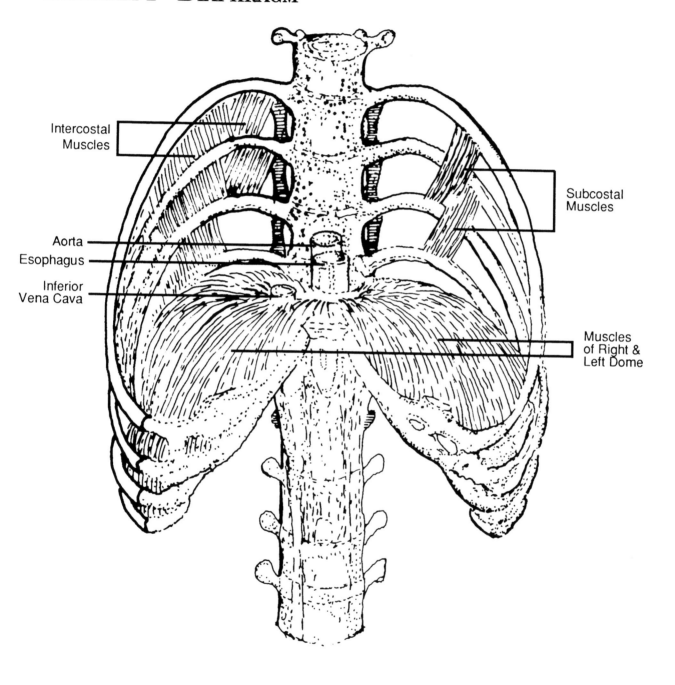

Intercostal
Muscles

Subcostal
Muscles

Aorta

Esophagus

Inferior
Vena Cava

Muscles
of Right &
Left Dome

Diagram 2 - Inhalation

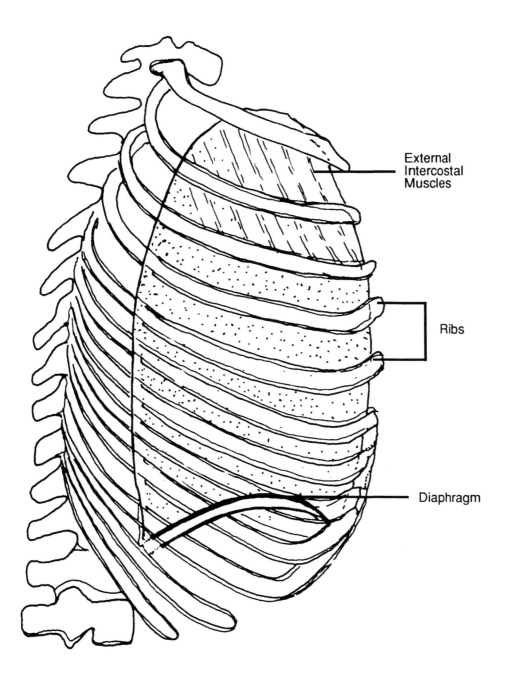

External
Intercostal
Muscles

Ribs

Diaphragm

DIAGRAM 3 - EXHALATION

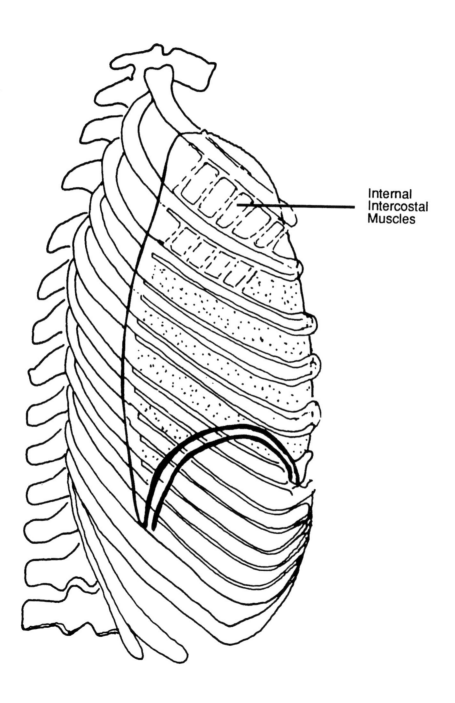

Internal
Intercostal
Muscles

2. CHORAL TECHNIQUES

Successful choral techniques begin in the mind of the director, developed in response to the choral sound of the ensemble, and are perfected only after progressive growth takes place within the context of the choral rehearsal. The director clearly sets the standard and that role can never be over-emphasized. Wilhelm Ehmann, in his book Choral Directing, states:

"In everything which the director does, whether actively or passively, he should always bear in mind that there is hardly another life situation in which the example of the leader has such an all-inclusive and shaping influence as in a choral situation." (EHMANN P. 209)

In this chapter, we will approach the tasks of the director that enable him or her to prepare for the choral experience in an organized and thoughtful way. We will attempt to answer the following questions:

- How is good communication best achieved?

- How are the problems of auditions and seating overcome?

- How may the chorus be trained through group vocalization?

- What is the best use of rehearsal time?

- What are the non-musical factors that influence our work?

- How can the choral curriculum be improved by planning and assessment?

When questions are raised and answers evolve, new ideas and more questions arise. An important point is that while each question may be addressed individually, the actual experience of working in a choral environment involves a multitude of ideas, theories, concepts and skills, each influencing the others.

COMMUNICATION WITH SINGERS

Communication is constant and on-going. It may be positive or negative, active or passive, musical or non-musical. Successful conductors are sensitive to the fact that if anything musical is going to happen in the allotted time, it must be planned, initiated and directed. Secondary school choral singers are volunteers.... They have chosen to be there for a number of reasons: social, personal or musical. The conductor should never forget that music is only one of a myriad of interests, activities or responsibilities of the chorister. Keeping music in its proper curricular perspective, though challenging, is important for all concerned parties (SINGLETON AND ANDERSON, P. 91).

THE ROLE OF THE CONDUCTOR

Motivational psychology should be working in every rehearsal. The role of the conductor is consistently that of motivating fine choral performance which aids in the development of pride and satisfaction among the adolescent singers. Individual achievement and the combined peer success within the group each contribute to positive motivation. These aforementioned behaviors on the part of adolescents are supported by research to the extent that they fall within the category of "self-actualization" (ABELES, HOFFER AND KLOTMAN, CH. 7). Whereas the chorister may be present for social reasons (extrinsic) or for musical reasons (intrinsic), the important point is the chorister is <u>present</u> and interested in choral participation.

Perhaps it is best to describe ideal characteristics of good communication skills in actual behavioral terms and what a conductor does in order to foster positive communication. Consider the following:

- Be aware of a limited attention-span. Be ready for a change in activity every 8-10 minutes.

- Waste no time. Be precise in directions. Talk less—sing more.

- Always stand up during rehearsals. A seated conductor does not command the attention of the choristers.

- Look for opportunities to be a positive reinforcer. Praise works better than censure.

- Maintain eye contact consistently. Know the musical score so well that you can look at the singers.

- Be alert to group dynamics. Utilize humor as a teaching strategy when an opportunity arrives.

- Generate enthusiasm, confidence and enjoyment. Build success on success.

-Model the melodic line or the tone quality desired. Demonstrate musically what is expected.

- Never underestimate visual cues. Body language speaks as clearly as the voice. Be conscious of conducting patterns and what they really mean.

- Utilize the audio tape recorder and/or the video camera to analyze group dynamics and musical results of your rehearsal time. Use them for self-evaluation.

A longer list could certainly be developed. The emphasis here is on positive, optimistic and well-prepared leadership. Ultimately, the conductor must inspire the singers to develop loyalty to their ensemble and to take pride in what they sing. The line between teacher and/or conductor is deceptive; the role may change from moment to moment during a rehearsal. Experienced teacher/conductors know that in the on-going work of choral singing, teaching and learning must occur or a piece will never be sung well. The changing role of the teacher/conductor will be discussed later in this chapter.

The product of the rehearsals — the performance— will genuinely reflect the skills and the ear of the conductor; but in the area of communication within the context of good education in music, it will also represent positive rapport and adolescent fulfillment.

MEETING THE SINGERS :
INTERVIEWS

Meeting the singers for the first time is usually done in a group setting. Junior and senior high school class schedules rarely provide for individual appointments. However, the conductor must take the time to schedule each singer for a private meeting in order to become acquainted with the voice. There is, of course, something to be learned from group singing from the start. Several group meetings early in the season will build confidence, develop rapport and actually allow the singers to "sing-through" most of the audition material. This strategy, though time consuming, may well be an advantage in the long run (BOYD, Ch. 3). The technique or system of interviewing and auditioning young singers is entirely dependent on the philosophy of the conductor and the school. If the choral organizations are open to all, regardless of ability, based upon interest only, group classification may be appropriate and the conductor can learn a great deal by vocalizing each section rather than individuals. If, on the other hand, the philosophy of the school encourages a select choir among its choral organizations, it is a necessity to interview and audition each singer who wishes to participate. It should be acknowledged that regardless of auditions and seating arrangements, the quality of the voices will be constantly changing throughout the season as a result of physical maturity combined with vocal practice. Flexibility in seating is essential if the choral ensembles are to grow in musicianship. For the purposes described in this chapter, the authors highly recommend individual interviews and auditions in any choral ensemble, perhaps several times during the year.

AUDITIONS / SELECTION

The purpose of an audition (or "tryout") is to learn all one can about the qualities of the voice and the nature of the personality of the singer. As in the performance of all music, nothing occurs in isolation. Many factors are at work simultaneously in the vocal mechanism and numerous musical ingredients come together to make up the performance of the singer. The conductor must listen for: tone quality (timbre), placement, diction, intonation and pitch, range, breath support, vibrato, phrasing, rhythm, dynamics and general musicianship. A recommended sequence is as follows (FENTON, XXI, No. 7):

1. Converse informally. Carry on a discussion about anything in order to listen to the speaking voice of the singer. What is the obvious timbre of the voice? What are the qualities of speech: diction, enunciation, pronunciation, style? Ask the singer to describe other musical experiences, thereby hearing the voice and at the same time learning more about the individual.

2. Vocalize the voice. Utilize a progressive set of vocalises that allows the singer to have immediate success, building confidence. Move from easy to difficult in order to judge the range of the voice and other factors. See illustrations below.

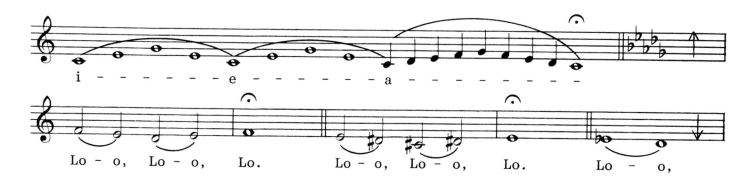

3. Match pitches (echo). Used primarily to test the ear of the singer and the ability to respond to changing pitch. Play on a <u>well-tuned</u> piano several intervals or short sequences, asking the singer to sing them back, in return.

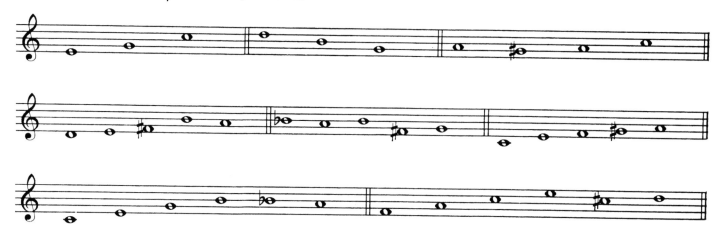

4. Sing a familiar folk song. Perhaps this song has already been rehearsed and sung in a large group, therefore it might not be as challenging as it could be. However, it will give the singer an opportunity to sing something familiar in confidence. Recommended songs for this segment are: <u>All Through the Night</u>, <u>Drink to Me Only With Thine Eyes</u>, and <u>Long, Long Ago</u>. Transpose as needed in order to allow each voice to sound in a comfortable tessitura and range.

5. Sight read several phrases from different styles and selections. These samples should be short and progressive, easy to difficult. Reading a part (soprano, alto, tenor or bass) from a choral score is sometimes effective with the piano playing a contrasting line. For example, a baritone singing his part against the piano playing other parts, omitting the baritone. An important facet of evaluating sight reading is the improvement in reading that might be demonstrated by a repeat performance. How well does the singer improve after the first reading?

With a well-planned sequence, the actual time commitment should be 10-12 minutes for each student. Some conductors recommend using a tape recorder in order to go back later to make final decisions. If this is done, logistics need to be planned carefully in order not to delay the schedule of singers waiting to be heard (ROE, Ch. 2). In any case, record-keeping is essential. A sample data card (5" x 8") is shown below which may be helpful in summarizing the interview/audition. There should always be an allowance for other factors. For example, the personality of the singer is important (shy, timid, curt, aggressive, pleasant, and so forth). A certain flair for precocity is sometimes welcomed by conductors (FENTON, XLVIII, No. 3). An awareness of the academic achievement of the singer may also be important. Whereas personality and academic achievement may not be deciding factors, they are part of the life and style of the singer and an awareness of them may assist the conductor in the weeks that follow. Clearly, the musical performance that results from the work in the rehearsal room is a combination of efforts brought about by cooperation. The conductor must realize that the singer is not just a voice, but a person as well. With a concern for the individual within the group, the conductor can also use the interview/audition experience to motivate the singer positively as the school year begins.

NAME _____ DATE _____

ADDRESS _____ PHONE _____

School Year: 6 7 8 9 10 11 12 (Circle One)

Musical Experience: _____

AUDITION NOTES:

Scale

Vocalization 1 2 3 4 5 Timbre _____
Pitch Matching 1 2 3 4 5 Placement _____
Folk Song 1 2 3 4 5 Diction _____
Sight Reading 1 2 3 4 5 Intonation _____
Comments: _____ Range _____
_____ Breath Support _____
_____ Vibrato _____
_____ Phrasing _____
_____ Rhythm _____
_____ Dynamics _____

SEATING

Seating arrangements for choral ensembles should be designed with flexibility in mind. The conductor will want to make changes as the acoustical need arises. When the voices mature, and the choral sound evolves with practice, change is inevitable. The singers should be prepared for that, in advance, so that it becomes normal procedure. Indeed, some recommendations include a variety of arrangements, based upon the type of composition being sung (EHMANN, Ch. 1). The majority of conductors agree on the basic principles of acoustics as their primary criterion for seating. How do the voices blend, one with the other? How many singers are there in each section? What are the variations in height? Who are the strongest musicians and how can they best help their peers? What are the varieties and styles of music to be performed? How mature and experienced are the singers? Care should be taken when making assignments in seating. The physical location of the voices will have a major impact on the devlopment of the "characteristic sound" of the ensemble.

Let us examine several typical seating arrangements and list their advantages.

#1

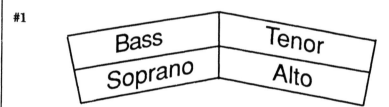

This arrangement has the advantage of the extreme voices (bass-soprano) together, so that intonation might be improved and sustained, particularly in the tuning of octaves. In addition, the inner voices (tenor-alto) are often written as partners and need to work together. This plan works especially well with small ensembles.

#2

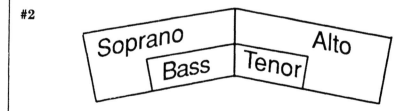

In this arrangement, the male voices are forward and centered, surrounded by larger numbers of female voices. This is particularly helpful if the number of voices is out-of-balance. With the bass-soprano and tenor-alto voices adjacent to one another, it has the same acoustical advantage as arrangement #1. In addition, if the number of male singers is smaller, it provides a psychological boost when tenor and bass sing in unison.

#3

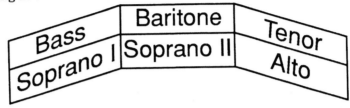

This arrangement is a variation of arrangement #1 as a result of a need for a larger choir with multiple parts to sing. It still keeps the high soprano and the low bass adjacent for intonation purposes. Obviously, an extension of this arrangement would be as follows, in order to accommodate 8-part singing.

#4

Bass	Baritone	Tenor II	Tenor I
Soprano I	Soprano II	Alto I	Alto II

The placement of female voices moves from low to high (right to left) and the male voices from low to high (left to right). For a variety of sound, if male voices are out-numbered, the reverse arrangement could be used, as shown below.

#5

Soprano I	Soprano II	Alto I	Alto II
Bass	Baritone	Tenor II	Tenor I

Please note, that in all arrangements, the semi-circular design is recommended. The voices should be directed toward the conductor as a central focus point. A choral ensemble should never sing in a straight line unless it is a very large choral unit (200+) voices with a symphony orchestra.

A more sophisticated type of arrangement is the scattered or mixed style with quartets rather than sections. While there are some advantages to this arrangement, the singers must be independently assured and musically strong. It is most appropriate in the singing of madrigals and motets for smaller ensembles, although some conductors use the scattered arrangement in multiple rows for larger works, as well.

#6

Arrangement #6 depicts a selective madrigal singing ensemble made up of: sopranos-6, altos-4, tenors-4, basses-5. There are six sopranos because madrigals and motets are often voiced as S-S-A-T-B. Varieties of this scattered arrangement may be used with larger groups, depending upon the abilities of the singers and the acoustical taste of the conductor's ear. For a more extensive discussion of the qualities and style of varied arrangements, reference is made of several leading writers (DECKER AND HERFORD, Ch. 2; EHMANN, Ch. 1; HEFFERNAN, Ch. 4; ROE, Ch. 2).

VOCALIZATION

Choral singing is a result of a number of functions taking place simultaneously. The physical action of the vocal mechanism combined with mental control and artistic expression should produce the desired result—a good choral sound. As part of the training of the vocal mechanism, the singers should be involved regularly in a variety of vocal exercises (vocalises). The importance of these exercises should not be overlooked by a conscientious conductor. Over a sustained period of time, a choral ensemble develops what could be called a "characteristic sound" that identifies them. Whether intentional or not, planned or happenstance, the "characteristic sound" becomes the musical trademark of the ensemble. Vocalises need to be carefully planned by the conductor to serve several purposes. They usually take place at the opening of the rehearsal but should also be sung if they can serve a pedagogical purpose within the workings of a composition. Exercising the voice through a vocalise begins the process of musical thinking. Truly, choral singing can often be compared with an athletic event even though the muscular effort and control are not as visible. One writer indicates that there are 130 parts of the body at work during the act of singing (HAMMAR, Ch. 9). Within the concept of human intelligence, Jean Piaget suggests that intelligence is identical with development, especially as combined with active learning—the involvement of the learner in the experience. Human intelligence, musically speaking, contains within it the capacity to interact with others, to control intonation and tone and to construct musical phrases (FURTH, P. 140).

The main purpose of a choral vocalise is to hear voices in a group setting, working toward exercising the vocal mechanism, in a healthy way and improving the sound, day by day, week by week, over a long period of time. Consistency is important so that progress can be measured based upon practice. Although vocalises may be designed to achieve a specific goal, as indicated earlier, nothing really occurs in isolation. One cannot improve intonation without producing good tone; good tone will not be produced without proper breath support; good breath support needs good posture; and so forth. When the singers know why they are vocalizing, they become intrinsically motivated to achieve specific goals and to measure their own improvement. In addition to exercising the vocal mechanism, vocalises can improve blend and balance, intonation, diction, breath support, timbre and placement, range, phrasing, rhythm, dynamics and general musicianship. Secondary results might include the measurement of ensemble progress, the prediction of what is to follow in a given rehearsal, the testing for acoustic properties in a different environment, and perhaps most important of all, the motivation for the singers to continually improve—to make them ready for a rehearsal or a performance. Examples of exercises that have met with reasonable success are as follows (FENTON, XVIX No. 2). IPA symbols are indicated by brackets in the text.

1. <u>Mee-May-Mah-Moh-Moo</u> [mi-me-mɑ-mo-mu]
Sing the diatonic scale ascending and descending in unison octaves no stronger than mezzo-piano (mp). The order of the vowels permits the "ee" [i] to be placed "forward" through the hard palate, encouraging the other vowels to follow. As the sequence rises chromatically with repetition, it causes the singers to experience the register changes from chest to middle to head registers with emphasis on the "oo" [u] sound and "forward" placement. This vocalise should also be sung as a canon. Easily done in a 2-part canon (women/men), it should be expanded to four parts (SATB) with the higher voices entering first: soprano, alto, tenor and then bass. The canonic experience will aid the singers in blend and intonation, particularly when sung no stronger than mezzo-piano (mp).

#1

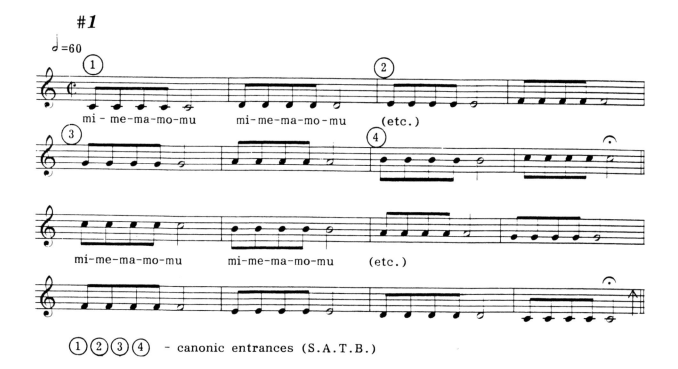

mi - me-ma-mo-mu   mi-me-ma-mo-mu   (etc.)

mi-me-ma-mo-mu   mi-me-ma-mo-mu   (etc.)

①②③④ - canonic entrances (S.A.T.B.)

2. <u>Mee-May-Mah</u> [mi-me-ma]
This sequence should begin quietly and in a moderate tempo. It should
be sung in unison octaves and four measures in one breath. It proceeds
from a comfortable pitch (E flat) and moves chromatically upward, until
the range limits are reached. As the sequence moves upward a
crescendo is logical and, of course, more breath support is needed. This
vocalise also provides the singers with the opportunity to tune octaves
and to concentrate on an accurate major third.

#2

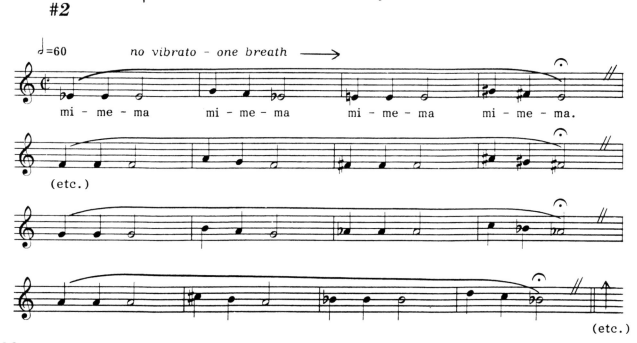

mi - me - ma   mi - me - ma   mi - me - ma   mi - me - ma.

(etc.)

(etc.)

3. <u>Dah-May-Nee-Poh-Too-Lah-Bay-Dah-May</u>

[da-me-ni-po-tu-la-be-da-me]

The use of the familiar Italian syllables has a particular purpose in this vocalise. It is done S.A.T.B. in a definite rhythmic pattern, closing on the "may" [me] sound (as in <u>neigh</u>-bor). Each sequence must be produced in one breath, rising chromatically at the end of the sequence, which places a demand on good intonation when the breath supply is nearly gone. When the last sequence is completed, the last "May" [me] descends chromatically, without apparent breath, changes vowels, and closes on the humming consonant "N" [n] with the lips slightly apart, sustaining a fermata with the conductor. It not only demands good breath control and support because of the diminuendo, but also crisp diction and precise intonation. In a diminuendo, more breath support is always needed, almost as if it were a crescendo. Parallel intervals (octaves, Major thirds, minor thirds, minor sixths, Perfect fourths and fifths) may all be heard simultaneously ascending and descending. The singers learn to concentrate on intonation and to practice "staggered" breathing.

etc., until reaching E ♭, then descend:

4. <u>Scale in unison with cadence</u>

Again, the use of the Italian syllables can create an excellent vocalise in diction and breath control. These syllables should be sung as quietly and as rapidly as possible with the rhythmic pattern <u>changing the accent</u> on each degree of the scale. A crescendo should occur toward the last "dah" [dɑ], causing the singers not only to accomplish precise diction, but also breath control, support and "forward" placement. The pattern should repeat in a descending fashion with a diminuendo at the closing. When the degrees of scale arrive at the tonic, the ensemble sings a chord sequence (S.A.T.B.) I-IV-I-V-I, with a fermata on each chord, closing quietly and in excellent control for balance, tone, breath and vowel purity. It is also an excellent place to practice staggered breathing, simulating sustained tone throughout the chord sequence.

5. <u>Cascading Scale Sequence</u>
Sing ascending and descending major scale in unison octaves on the syllable "May" [me] or "Mah" [ma]. Each voice sustains on a different scale tone as the scale descends, thus creating a harmonic structure for a closing cadence. This vocalise helps develop breath control, intonation, blend, balance and musical discipline within the choral ensemble.

#5

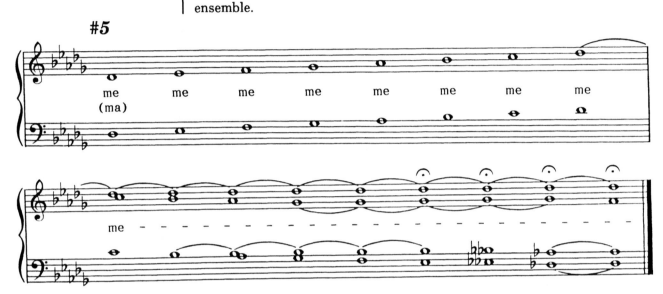

6. <u>Mee-May-Mah-Moh-Moo</u> [mi-me-ma-mo-mu] (Male voices)
This vocalise is a repetition of #1 with the exception that it is used to assist male singers in changing from the middle register to the head voice. The "oo" [u] vowel is emphasized near the end of the sequence in order to "lift" the voice into the head without strain, to find the pitch, and to experience head resonance, which may also go into falsetto. The male voices can be bolstered in resonance by adding the female voices to the vocalise in the <u>last two</u> measures of the ascending scale each time on the <u>exact true pitch</u> and completing the "oo" [u] sequence together. Vocalizing over the "break" into the upper register should also be practiced in a descending pattern, shown in illustration #7. The change in registers, sometimes called the "passagio", must be approached by both ascending and descending patterns.

#6

soprano/alto enter here

7. <u>Pur-Pur-Pur-Pur</u> [pur] (Male voices)
Specifically designed to sing from the middle to the high register, this vocalise also calls upon the female voices to bolster the resonance. The sopranos and altos join the tenors and basses on the <u>exact true pitch</u> as the sequence rises chromatically; the female voices should enter with ease and without strain. This vocalise can, when used correctly, allow the male voices to reach high Bb-B without strain, singing forward-on the breath-falsetto-in the head voice. The combination of #6 (ascending) and #7 (descending) will aid in the development of the male register change from the middle register into the head voice.

8. <u>HALLELUIA</u> [ha-le-lu-ja]
Sung in a straight-forward style in a descending major scale, rising chromatically in sequence, this vocalise calls upon the diaphragm to support the breath as it goes higher in pitch. The placement of the "oo" [u] vowel forward can assist the "ah" [a] vowel in also seeking the same forward placement. The use of the "H" [h] as a beginning consonant emphasizes the diaphragm breathing.

9. <u>Use of Glissando</u>
By singing the "N" [n] at the beginning of each sequence, sliding an octave in glissando, the "AH" [ɑ] vowel is place "in the mask" and permitted to achieve forward resonance. In addition, it calls for strong breath support as the sequence rises chromatically.

#9

10. <u>Loosening the Jaw</u>
By singing the syllable "YAH" [jɑ] vigorously throughout the vocalise, the jaw is caused to loosen and relax. Additionally, the "AH" [ɑ] vowel should, once again, be placed forward.

#10

In singing any of the vocalises illustrated above, a meaningful concept of tone needs to be in "the mind's ear" of the singer (HOLST, P. 8). This mental imagery is as much a working part of the voice as the vocal mechanism itself. To achieve a good choral sound, a uniformity of resonance must be found even though the individual voices are unique, one to another. How does the conductor accomplish this task? One of the best methods is by modeling the tone—demonstrating acceptable vowel sounds and tonal placement. As discussed in an earlier chapter, the singer needs to know the mechanism of the vocal apparatus in order to function properly within the ensemble. The conductor takes that knowledge and interprets the ingredients of "imagery" in order to get the desired sound. To the extent to which the process is successful, the ensemble develops its "characteristic sound" or choral trademark. Imagery takes on the use of words and phrases to represent timbre. Such terms as: "Spinning the tone", "lift" into the higher register, sing "forward in the mask", "brighten" the vowel, "darken" the vowel, sing "on the breath", focus the tone "straight-as-an-arrow", and so forth all lend themselves linguistically to the use of metaphor in order to communicate the type of sound the conductor is seeking. When that sound is accomplished, and the conductor's ear finally approves, the act of vocalizing serves as a reinforcement of style as well as a pedagogical tool. Verbal imagery and its use become the bridge from vocalization to performance.

Throughout the experience of vocalization the emphasis is on the correct forward resonance and phonation of the vowel sounds EE-AY-AH-OH-OO [i-e-ɑ-o-u] as found in the Italian language. In his book <u>SINGING - AN EXTENSION OF SPEECH</u>, Russell Hammar categorizes this sequence as "the vowel spectrum", going into great detail on the physiological function of the vocal mechanism during vocalization (HAMMAR, Ch. 3). Modifications of these vowels aid the ensemble in accomplishing the blending of voices and the improvement of intonation. The fact is that the exercises shown above cannot be sung properly without breath support, crisp diction, and correct placement of the tone. Ultimately, the sustaining of the choral "line" is dependent on the proper placement and the articulation of consonants from syllable to syllable, word to word, thereby completing a musical phrase.

To summarize the art of vocalization, the following should be considered:

- There should always be a purpose for vocalizing.

- The emphasis should be on the voice and listening: minimize the use of a piano.

- The singers should stand while singing. Chairs should be in place for an occasional rest; however, standing presents the best posture.

- Allow the singers to stand apart from one another. If they are crowded together, the skill of listening is hindered.

- Vocalize progressively from easy to challenging, so that the singers may experience success.

- Reinforce the concept of tonality by utilizing the syllables of moveable-do and scalewise numbers from time to time.

-Be aware that the inner hearing of the singer is not always in tune with the actual tone production.

- Sustain the vowel as soon as possible. Use consonants as connectors.

- Be aware of vibrato. Determine the extent to which it will or will not be part of the "characteristic sound" of the ensemble.

- Remember that singing in unison usually means unison <u>octaves</u>.

- Vocalization should allow the voice to function freely, without strain, with the dynamics moderate in amplitude.

- Develop the upper register with a series of descending major scales.

- Time allotted for vocalization should not exceed 5-7 minutes in a regularly scheduled rehearsal.

REHEARSALS

As we leave the topic of choral vocalizing, it is most logical to move into the structure of the rehearsal. Rehearsal, as a word, literally means to "re-hear" or to repeat in practice in order to perform. We are all so accustomed to the word that no serious thought is usually given to its definition. In order to "re-hear", we must first "hear" and continue to hear in a progressive way throughout a sequence of rehearsals aimed toward a performance goal. Excellent performances do not just happen; they are the results of planning and preparation on the part of the conductor and the ensemble in partnership. The rehearsal climate or environment should be a positive one in which a variety of choral experiences take place. Ever conscious of the attention-span of chorus members, conductors should provide the singers with interesting and challenging things to do. Above all, the momentum of active involvement in singing should be sustained.

The main objective in any rehearsal is problem-solving. As choral techniques improve and singers gain experience, the problems are narrowed down, but they are always present. Conductors must decide which problems are more demanding than others, which to approach first and how to go about it. Indeed, by solving some problems early, others may be eliminated. A timetable of emphasis on problem-solving is best illustrated with the following chart:

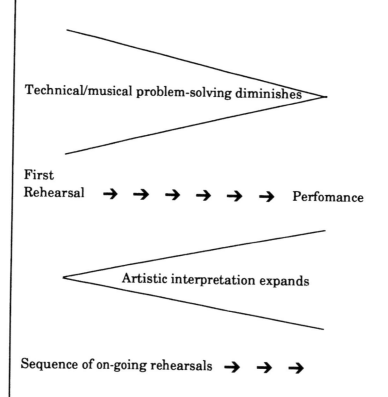

Technical/musical problem-solving diminishes

First
Rehearsal → → → → → → Perfomance

Artistic interpretation expands

Sequence of on-going rehearsals → → →

In the illustration above, the emphasis in the early rehearsals is on the solving of technical and musical problems (tone, breath, pitch, intonation, diction, and so forth) with little or no emphasis on artistic interpretation. The director is a teacher more than a conductor. As time goes by, be it eight days or eight weeks—the proportion of time spent remains the same—the artistic interpretation becomes the emphasis. This can only occur, of course, if all the technical and musical problems have been solved along the way. At this point, the conducting is emphasized as a result of good teaching. Clearly, the teacher/conductor role changes day by day. An important point to make here is this: at the last minute (or last rehearsal) it is not really wise to try to solve a technical or musical problem. The error has already been learned. Once the interpretation-learning dominates the rehearsal, the technical and musical problems regrettably become part of the product—the performance.

Planning and preparation for rehearsals are essential elements for success as a choral conductor. Rehearsals should be progressive, time after time, so that something is always accomplished. It is the evaluation of this accomplishment that the conductor uses as a basis for planning ahead, step by step. Score study is essential. The conductor should know every part, sing every part, play the score at the piano in order to inter-relate the parts, and anticipate possible problems. By anticipation, for example, an appropriate vocalise may be selected to approach a problem that may arise. Probably one of the most important things a conductor can do to prepare for rehearsal is to completely understand the music, both technically and, as a work of literature. Too often, we forget that choral music incorporates prose or poetry which has meaning and is to be communicated to an audience of listeners. The serious conductor will look upon the preparation for rehearsal as a major responsibility (HEFFERNAN, Ch. 2).

ELEMENTS OF A GOOD REHEARSAL

There is general agreement among several choral writers about the activities that should take place in a good rehearsal. Generally, the order is this: vocalize, sing a familiar piece, introduce a new piece or work on a piece in progress, and close with another familiar piece that has been recently learned (BEESON, TATARUNIS and FORCUCCI, Ch. 12; BOYD, Ch. 5, 6; EHMANN, Ch. B5; ROE, Ch. 9; SINGLETON and ANDERSON, Ch. 6). For the purposes of this chapter, we suggest the following sequence of events that should take place in an efficient, musical rehearsal, keeping in mind that in addition to managing time, the conductors must always work toward positive motivation and seek musical results:

1. Vocalization (5-7 minutes).

2. First selection - well-liked, familiar, successful (3-4 minutes).

3. Second selection - The most difficult piece of the day; perhaps a review of an on-going work phrase by phrase, section by section. Iron out difficulties in smaller segments (10-12 minutes).

4. Third and Fourth selections - Review earlier works that are now ready for "run-through" refinement. Introduce new works or insert ear-training or sight reading component (10-12 minutes).

5. General announcements (2-3 minutes). Never place announcements at the beginning of a rehearsal.

6. Last selection - Close rehearsal with highly positive, well-known piece. Leave the rehearsal in an optimistic frame of mind (3-4 minutes).

This sequence utilizes a maximum of forty-two minutes, based upon the assumption that the typical junior or senior high school class is forty-five minutes in length.

One of the basic skills of a good conductor is the ability to "tear down" and "build up" a musical score line by line, section by section, phrase by phrase, measure by measure, until it is finally ready for the synthesis called performance. A system for such strategy is described in the following outline.

Rehearsing a new selection:

1. Conductor (or accompanist) plays through entire piece at moderate tempo. Optional humming (using [ŋ]) or soft singing with text or neutral syllable [lu, lu, lu] takes place. Singers conduct the meter with teacher, thereby, involving singers in movement, listening and singing in order to assist them in "internalizing" the new selection.

2. Sing through the entire selection at a moderate tempo. If the rhythm is complex, oral reading of the text is appropriate before singing. Sing through regardless of errors the first time; don't stop. Do not sing through again, however, until step #8.

3. Point out all important factors before proceeding: tempo changes, key changes, rhythmic problems, diction, phrasing, and so forth.

4. Begin to work on the entrance section as the first project. How does the piece begin?

5. Begin to work on the closing section as the next phrase. How does the piece end?

6. Work on the most difficult section and connect it to easier neighboring sections. There is a detailed discussion of this procedure by Lloyd Pfautsch in the book: CHORAL CONDUCTING: A SYMPOSIUM, edited by Harold Decker and Julius Herford (DECKER and HERFORD, Ch. 2).

7. Work in reverse, adding and joining one section at a time through to the learned ending section each time, thereby reinforcing previously worked material. This procedure will develop musical continuity and assist in breath control and phrasing.

8. Add the learned entrance section to the worked and re-worked middle sections through to the learned ending section. This is the first time the piece has been "sung-through" since the first reading (step #2).

9. Polish for all factors and stress interpretation.

Throughout the basic "tear-down" and "build-up" of the score, there is a hierarchy of decision-making going on in the mind of the conductor. Consider the order as one in which all factors are certainly dependent on one another; however, there is a certain priority if followed, that will save rehearsal time and, in the end, improve the musicianship of the ensemble.

THE CONDUCTOR'S EAR

The ear of the conductor determines what is acceptable. In listening to the ensemble in the early stages of rehearsal, the following order of problem-solving is recommended:

1. Rhythm and pitch

2. Phrasing and breath support

3. Tone and blend

4. Text and diction

5. Dynamics

In other words, the dynamics of a piece cannot really be properly achieved until all other factors have been accomplished. Each of these factors influence each other and certainly nothing can be isolated to the exclusion of all others. However, the main point in hierarchial thinking is that there are priorities that must be determined by the conductor and that the logical approach to those priorities in sequence will assist the ensemble in accomplishing much in a minimum amount of time. To cite two examples of decision-making: a slower tempo in rehearsal in order to secure rhythm and diction may temporarily sacrifice good phrasing, but may be necessary; trying to balance dynamics too soon may sacrifice tone, blend and intonation. This description of the craft of learning a composition leads to the final result of rehearsal—the performance.

Ancillary to every good rehearsal plan will be the elements of voice class, ear-training and sight reading. In other chapters in this book, these topics are discussed at length. However, it is worth noting here that the actual skills should be interspersed into a rehearsal plan regularly. The most logical place would be in step #4 where new material may be introduced. The involvement of actually sight reading printed music selections is an important facet of learning the skill. Daily practice and drill, with the use of syllables and/or numbers as well as letter names will be rewarded, over time. Sight reading and ear-training go hand in hand and daily practice is essential, so that the concepts of tonality and rhythm may be constantly reinforced through a variety of keys, tempi and style. For a list of supplementary materials, refer to Chapter I, REALIZING THE POTENTIAL OF YOUNG SINGERS and Chapter IV, EAR-TRAINING.

REHEARSAL REMINDERS

In leaving the topic of rehearsal, the following list of general reminders may help the conductor in planning for the best use of rehearsal time:

- Always start and end on time. Set an example and expect the same in return.

- Musical learning within the rehearsal must be active and experiential, never passive. Talk less—sing more.

- Never repeat a section or an exercise without cause; always explain why.

- Do not sing with the ensemble. Inner hearing will interfere with discriminate listening.

- Respect the voice as a physical instrument.

- Stand for rehearsal most of the time, with chairs available when needed.

- Try to avoid rehearsing errors. Catch them early.

- Stress "a capella" singing, even in rehearsal. Avoid too much reliance on the piano, which should not be a model for pitch or tone.

- Sing from memory as early as possible. This not only helps with vocal production and increases attentiveness, it also aids in internalizing the music (EHMANN, Ch. B-V).

- Vary the rehearsal to avoid monotony; alternate tempi, key, style, mood, languages and context.

- Maintain eye contact with singers to constantly improve communication.

- Involve singers in conducting. Teach the basic patterns. Utilize student conductors.

- Improve diction by speaking the text; especially helpful when working with counterpoint.

- Use neutral syllables [lu,lu,lu] instead of text in difficult passages, particularly in foreign languages.

- Model the tone and style for the ensemble. Let them imitate.

- Refrain from conducting occasionally during the polishing stage; rely on the ears, causing the ensemble to listen to one another; turn singers facing away from conductor; change positions on stage; move while singing; force singers to listen—all at a late stage of development when all parts are learned and interpretation is the goal.

- Rehearse in one large circle, facing center; rehearse in four circles (S - A-T-B); rehearse in four circles in quartets.

- Involve singers in the support of part-learning for "other" parts. Double the parts; rehearse common parts together: line, rhythm, text, unison; rehearse outer parts together (S-B); inner parts (A-T); male parts (T-B); female parts (S-A); higher parts (S-T); lower parts (A-B), and so forth as they may be in common, building phrases from a single line up to full harmonic texture.

- Improve the clarity of diction and rhythm by changing tempo occasionally. Reduce the tempo in a rapid piece or increase the tempo in a slow piece (at first) to assist in phrasing and long breath development. In other words, change the tempo to solve the problem, gradually returning to the correct tempo.

- Remember the "law of diminishing returns"—the arrival at a point at which the performance of a skill begins to worsen. Don't over-rehearse. The best use of rehearsal time seems to be from 5-12 minutes on a single task. Anticipate change.

- On the day of a performance, have the singers read the text of each piece before going on stage. This makes it possible for the performance itself to not be the first time that day the text has crossed their minds.

- Demand the best effort from the ensemble, but be prepared to give your best effort in return.

CHANGING VOICES

A book on choral musicianship or a chapter on choral techniques would be incomplete without some commentary on changing voices. Much has been written on this topic and some researchers have gone into great detail to categorize the various stages of development experienced by young singers. It is important for the choral conductor to learn as much as possible about the mutation experience in the young child as he or she enters puberty and evolves as a young adult. It is equally important to realize that the biological change in the lives of young singers is not the only factor affecting the choral rehearsal. The psychological/social arena of pre-adolescent and adolescent behavior is one in which constant change and volatility should be expected. Anne Petersen, author of "Those Gangly Years" states:

"The biological events of puberty are a necessary—and largely uncontrollable—part of growing up."

The environment and the social forces, however, are often controllable. As teachers, we must nurture the activities of our students as maturity takes place (PETERSEN, P. 28)

The human voice is in a constant stage of development and change, but for our purposes, we are directing our attention to the junior high/ middle school years through which young adulthood is attained. The term "settled" has been used by a number of writers to indicate the end of the pubertal growth that results in a young adult voice. However, even at that stage, the process of change continues as the teenager matures. The choral director working with young voices needs to always nurture them carefully in order not to cause strain or injury.

In the late ninteenth century, Francis E. Howard, Supervisor of Music in Bridgeport, Connecticut, and a choirmaster of an all-male cathedral choir, wrote extensively on the use of the child voice. In his experience, his choir singers were clearly more advanced than singers in school settings; and it was primarily from his church choir orientation that he based his conclusions on the changing voice of young boys. His observations included: the speaking voice usually changed first; if the voice changed rapidly, all singing should stop; if the voice changed gradually, the boy should be allowed to "sing through the break"; and, if the boys sang through the various parts (alto and tenor), he would eventually become a tenor.

He was rather pragmatic about it, because in his church choir, he needed altos. A very practical demand caused him to encourage the continuance of singing, with the reservation to always be alert to guard against the misuse of the voice.

According to a survey of his own colleagues of choirmasters, the majority felt that singing through the change would cause injury to the voice and that the boy should stop singing when his voice "broke". It must be remembered that this attitude was a result of the strong English Cathedral tradition of choir training, where the alto line was sung primarily by counter-tenors. It seems quite apparent that no thought was ever given to the idea of arranging the music to suit the changing voice.

In summary, Howard's dilemma regarding the boy's changing voice can best be stated as follows:

"It is an unmanageable and unmusical voice, it is harsh, unsympathetic, hard to keep in tune, its presence in a choir is a constant menace to the soprano tone, and were it not for the idea that there is no recourse from this voice, save in the employment of women altos, it would not be tolerated by musicians" (HOWARD - Ch. 7, 8).

In the early twentieth century, Father William J. Finn began his long and eminent career as a choral conductor in the city of Chicago. Beginning in 1904, he developed a style of ecclesiastical all-male choral singing that commanded respect and attention wherever it was heard. By 1939, he was able to publish his system of choral singing and share it with others. He, too, felt that the obvious thing for a boy to do when his voice "broke" was to rest for two or three years. But, in order to avoid that loss of time, careful and extensive vocalization should take place in order to preserve the head voice and help develop the newly discovered lower voice. However, he avoided the middle register in his vocalization patterns. His primary concern seemed to be sustaining an equal quality of tone throughout the change because of the ungainly influence of the voice in polyphonic music and difficulty in blending within homophonic compositions. He supported the idea of singing through the change, first as an alto, then as a counter-tenor, with a consistent regard for tone quality and blend as a result of careful vocalization (FINN - Ch. 8).

Perhaps two of the most well-known researchers in the area of young voices are Irvin Cooper and Karl Kuersteiner. In 1965, they published one of the most respected volumes on junior high school music. Over a period of eight years, from 1939 - 1947, Irvin Cooper, as guest conductor or as workshop leader, came in contact with over 81,000 adolescent voices—both boys and girls. It was from this vast experience that his theories on voice classification evolved.

Cooper and Kuersteiner emphasized four stages of boy's changing voices: (1) Unchanged, (2) Cambiata (first change), (3) Baritone (second change), (4) Young adult baritone or tenor (bass-a rarity). They concluded that along with rare true basses, the true tenor did not exist in this age group. The tenor parts, as they were generally written, were too low, even though the range was similar to the projected Cambiata; the tessitura was incorrect for the changing boy's voice.

In order to identify the various voices, a group classification system evolved which has proven to be highly successful. Essentially, the Cambiata (changing) voice is discovered by the process of elimination; that is, in group singing, all baritones are identified, the key is changed and all sopranos are discovered, and; the remaining singers are those in the process of change—Cambiata. It seems, at first, that this system is unscientific. However, in the class (group) singing environment, it becomes workable. As in all choral work, the conductor's musical "ear" is crucial to success.

They were also concerned about the treatment of girl's voices during the same adolescent period of growth. They felt that there really was no such thing as a true soprano or alto voice at this time. Girls should sing in two equal groups, with parts rotated and counterpoint encouraged. The rotation of parts was important because it allowed all girls to use the full range of the voice and not fall into a soprano or alto designation too soon.

The influence of the Cooper-Kuersteiner methods and techniques cannot be over emphasized. There is never a doubt that "singing through" the change is not only acceptable, but essential; and that musical arrangements need to be written to accommodate the special needs of the voice during this growth period (COOPER AND KUERSTEINER, Ch. 3).

Paul F. Roe, in 1970, felt that it was not only normal to deal openly with the voice changes in students, but important to discuss it with them as the process took place. He considered four types of voices in the age of puberty: (1) the girl's voice, (2) the boy's unchanged voice, (3) the boy's changing voice, (4) the boy's changed voice. He, too, felt that the girl's voice parts should be rotated so that no soprano or alto designations be pre-determined; and, that the head voice and the chest register would not be forced, respectively. A proper pedagogical procedure, in his opinion, was to retain the upper range, develop the lower range and work from both into the middle register until they met (ROE - Ch. 7).

Eighty-two eighth grade boys were studied over a period of two semesters by Frederick J. Swanson, of the University of Wisconsin. In his research, he designed an individual voice testing procedure that measured the progress of voice mutation four times from September to May. As a result, he classified his boy singers into four categories: (1) treble only, (2) lower bass only, (3) two voices - treble and bass with a gap of silence between, (4) full range, with an overlap of two voices with some middle tones produced by either voice. The ranges of each boy were measured and graphed individually as the year progressed. Swanson was motivated in his research partly because he felt that the lack of interest in music shown by many junior high/middle school boys at the time of the biological activity of the mutation process was no coincidence. Since it was a normal part of growing up, it was wise to understand what was going on, turn it into an exciting and interesting time for the boy and, by careful planning, accommodate the vocal changes by grouping the singers. Indeed, the larger the group, the easier it was to manage. Continual testing allowed for rotating the singers among various groups as the changes occurred. Flexible class scheduling was essential to his plan. With the ability to alternate music classes with health, physical education and industrial arts classes, it made it possible for him to rotate the boys throughout the academic year.

An important part of his writing in 1973 was the stress he placed on the need for the teacher of music to be sincerely interested in the young student. One should never underestimate the psychological/social situation in which motivation plays such an important part. As far as the mutation process is concerned, although it is scientific, biological, physical, acoustical and musical, the psychological/social factors surrounding the rapport of the teacher and student are equally as important (SWANSON, Ch. 12, 13).

Through a series of articles in 1977-78, John M. Cooksey proposed an eclectic attitude toward solving the problem of the changing voice in boys. In his "Integrated Approach", he recommended both group and individual testing and that it be on-going throughout the school year. His experience, over the years, convinced him that there are, indeed, five stages of voice change for boys: (A) Pre-mutation (age 10-12), (B) Early mutation (age 12-13), (C) High Mutation (age 13-14), (D) Postmutational (age 14-17), (E) Early adult (age 17-18).

In addition, it was essential that the boys clearly understand the principles of tone production (phonation and breath support); and, that the voices were vocalized regularly throughout the various stages. Sensitivity to change, individual as well as group attention and small group singing were emphasized by Cooksey. His recommendations for grouping stressed flexibility and indicated that, among all the choices, eighth grade boys alone would be the most undesirable grouping. It would be better to have one large boy's chorus of grades 7-9 where flexibility would permit groups to be formed. His recommendation for mixed chorus at this age would be 8th and 9th grade combined (S-A-T-B) because he felt the voices were more "settled" and that better literature was available (COOKSEY, CHORAL JOURNAL, VOL. XVIII, NO. 2,3,4,5).

In each theory described above, it is clear that the experience of the particular proponent influences his point of view. The differences over the years are not as important as the ideas held in common. The following guidelines or general principles come to the surface:

- In the process of child development, during the mutation of the voice, the voice may change rapidly, erratically, gradually or spasmodically, and is difficult to predict

- Choral conductors need to be sensitive to change on a daily basis.

-The psychological/social factors are as important as musical factors.

- Cooperation with other teachers may assist the choral director in grouping classes (health, physical education, industrial arts).

- Singing through the change is encouraged, with careful vocalization.

- Selection of music should be based on range and tessitura.

- Girl's voices should not be categorized as soprano or alto too early.

- The speaking voice generally begins to change earlier than the singing voice.

- Testing and classification of the changing voices should be an on-going process.

- Unison singing in octaves should be avoided because of limited ranges.

- The changing voice is an integral part of the normal biological development of young people and can be approached in a positive way.

- Good tone production through vocalization should always be sought throughout the period of change.

- Choral directors need to be perpetual students in order to continue to learn about the problems of the changing voice and profit from the experience of others (see references at the end of this chapter).

The majority of junior high/middle school teachers will have in their music classes "all the children of all the people" and must work with some who sing, some who do not sing, some who have years of success in singing, and others who have rejected singing as a part of their lives. Frustration with the changing voice and with the combination of psychological/social factors combined have caused numerous music educators to avoid the age group and teach elsewhere. At the same time, for the same reasons, others are drawn to this age group and meet with much success. The teacher of choral music needs to be sincerely interested in the evolutionary environment of biological change in order to progressively work with the problems and achieve success.

NON-MUSICAL FACTORS

A conductor needs many talents and skills, some of them non-musical. The basic principles of time management, organization and personnel practices need to be accounted for. If a conductor feels that these attributes are not interesting or not part of acquired skills, then they should be delegated to others who may be relied upon. Simply put, the fine choral performances that everyone aspires to will not take place if logistic support is not functioning. As obvious as it may seem, it is worthwhile to review here.

The mechanics of management assume that the rehearsal room is large enough to house the ensemble in such a way that there is ample standing and sitting room and that there is enough cubic feet (with high ceilings) to allow for proper breathing and ventilation. This same factor of cubic feet also assists in the reverberation of choral sound so that members of the ensemble may hear each other as well as the conductor hears the total sound (GEERDES, Ch. 3). Along with space and ventilation, the important element of proper lighting needs attention. The cleanliness of the environment should also be a priority. Voices are human and vulnerable to sore throats, head colds and all manner of problems. Traffic areas need to be monitored. Much time is lost on busy days when there is a traffic jam getting in and out of a sloppy rehearsal room. Chairs, stands, music and folders all need to be accounted for so that the business of "getting started" and "finishing up" a rehearsal is not a daily experience in chaos. Attendance taking should be delegated to student leadership as in the case of music library work. Reliable students are highly motivated and can save the conductor mountains of grief. The order of rehearsal should be posted in a conspicuous location so that all singers may know what is expected upon walking into the room. Above all, the piano should be well-tuned and inspected frequently. Finally, the awareness of acoustics should be ever present. Control of reverberation is something that one learns from experience and by experimentation. Drapes to cut down the "echo" or reflective panels to enliven the sound are two examples of treatment. In the opinion of the authors, it is better to rehearse in an acoustically "dry" environment where everyone can hear; and perform in a "live" area where the sound may be enhanced and supported. Personal preference enters into these decisions and once again influences the "characteristic sound" of the ensemble. A successful performance is the result of a positive environment and careful planning.

In summary, the teaching/learning/ performance environment has certain desirable characteristics that show foresight and concern on the part of the conductor. This is a visible sign to the singers that "singing is our business" and we are now "ready to work".

PLANNING AND ASSESSMENT

Conductors are always involved in planning ahead, whether it is systematic or by instinct. Every occasion calls for anticipating, programming and working out all details before the final performance. Our purpose here is to discuss several distinct components that can influence the products of the choral experience—the performance and quality education in music: goal-setting (long-range planning); developing a rehearsal schedule toward a specific performance (short-range planning); and assessment through the planning process.

In the book FOUNDATIONS OF MUSIC EDUCATION, the authors, in their discussion of motivation, have this to say about establishing goals:

"Good teachers are able to guide their students, indicating their present position or starting point, their final destination, and alternative routes to their goals as well as providing sub-goals along the route that will allow for measurement of how much of the total distance has been traveled" (ABELES, HOFFER and KLOTMAN, P. 184).

In order for this type of guidance to take place, the "good teachers" need to have a complete overview of where they and their ensembles are going as working partners in choral performance. Some type of planning is essential in order to achieve a high level of quality assurance and musical growth.

What are reasonable goals? The Music Educators National Conference, in its second edition of THE SCHOOL MUSIC PROGRAM: DESCRIPTION AND STANDARDS, suggests that quality choral curricula for both junior high/middle school and senior high school include at least two choral units meeting daily with the membership based upon experience and ability as well as by units for girls, boys and mixed voices. An assumption is made by MENC that the class schedule is based on an eight-period day so that these opportunities are possible. In addition, at the high school level, at least one alternative choral unit for each 300 students should be offered. Such alternatives as madrigal singers, show choir, and ethnic choral groups are recommended, with the contingency that membership in such groups be limited to those who are already part of the larger choral units (MENC, P. 34-37).

Clearly, the school population and the class schedules (eight-period day) are two crucial factors in planning for curriculum development. Long-range planning always involves quantitative data; and, a longitudinal study of the student population growth over a five-year period would be very helpful indeed in projecting a possible expansion of a choral curriculum. How many students are expected to arrive at the various grade levels and when? What opportunities can be provided for them in choral music? How can they be scheduled within the school day so that everyone who wishes to participate may have the opportunity? How may these multiple units be accommodated in space, equipment, supplies and staff? What impact will this expanded long-range plan have on budgeting demands? All of these questions and others need to be addressed in sympathy with the established philosophy of music education that prevails in the individual school.

For the purposes of this chapter on choral techniques, we would suggest the following as an ideal choral curriculum in the senior high school:

- Select choral group (S-A-T-B)
An auditioned group of singers who are juniors and seniors. This group might be titled: a capella choir, chorale, singers.

- Chorus (S-A-T-B)
    Open to all juniors and seniors

- Sophomore choir (S-A-T-B)
    Open to all sophomores

- Freshman choir (S-A-T-B)
    Open to all freshmen

- Ancillary groups:
    Girls's ensemble (S-A, S-S-A, S-S-A-A)
    Boy's glee club (T-B, T-B-B, T-T-B-B)
    Vocal Jazz/Pop Ensemble (S-A-T-B)

- Solo and ensemble (ad hoc)
    An auditioned experience

- Choral Union
    Combined units in festival at least once each year.

- Voice class (see Chapter I)

For the junior high/middle school, our recommendation includes two choral units (S-A-T-B), but with additional concern for voicing that would be flexible, dependent upon the changing voices of young adolescents. Such groupings as S-A, S-S-A, high-medium-low, Cambiata-tenor-baritone, and S-S-Cambiata-baritone might be utilized throughout the academic year as the vocal demands change. And, for motivational purposes, the young adolescents generally respond to such titles as varsity choir, pop singers, middle-school musicians, and so forth, thereby claiming a unique identity with their peers.

Short-range planning takes place as a regular part of the school calendar of activities. At the beginning of the season, the conductor studies the calendar, chooses target dates for concert performances and begins to plan repertoire that probably can be achieved in the given period of time. If nothing else, this minimal experience in planning does take into account the number of hours of rehearsal available and the number of weeks between performances. In anticipation of the pre-determined concert date, the following sequence is recommended as the ensemble enters the final two weeks of preparation:

1. In the second week before the concert date, each individual piece is polished and grouped in sequence of keys, style, tempi and context. The program is formed and rehearsed in groups.

2. Five days before the concert, the ensemble performs a first "run-through" in the performance hall. A selected audience may be invited and a video or audio tape is made for review.

3. Three to four days before a concert performance, a review and rehearsal are conducted by groups of selections in order to reinforce the relationship of one to the other. Interpretation is polished.

4. Two days before the concert a final "run-through" or dress rehearsal takes place in the performance hall.

5. One day before the concert, rest the voices.

6. The day of the concert a light pre-concert vocalise should be sung and a briefing of logistics for the event should take place. Singers should verbally read through the text before going on stage, so that when they sing, it is not the first time they have recalled the words.

Assessment or evaluation is a vital part of any musical growth. Subjective judgement of the concert performances is expected of all who attend. School performances are appreciated and admired for a number of reasons: appropriate literature for young singers; a good, solid performance; enthusiasm for the ensemble and the school; and parental love for their children. The conductor should try to be as objective as possible and measure the product in educational and musical terms. How did it sound in comparison to other recent performances and to those of the previous year? Have certain vocal problems been overcome, or are they still present? Has the ensemble demonstrated any fluency in singing in any other language other than English? What was the audience response and how did it compare with other performances? These and other questions can assist the conductor in the next phase of planning that should occur immediately.

Assessment may be viewed best at the end of an academic year when the conductor can look back over the season and attempt to measure growth. Choral ensembles are usually at their best sound and maturity in April and May, closing out the year. When the next season begins, minus all graduating seniors, there is an inevitable drop in maturity and experience. However, as one year follows another, the "drop" at the beginning of the academic year should be at a higher level each year if the curriculum is developed that supports multiple ensembles and voice classes. The standard of quality is raised year by year for approximately four to five years before one can sense a "leveling-off" of growth. There is a limit to adolescent voices, but the quality that can be achieved in a carefully planned curriculum can be consistent, year after year.

Planning, whether it is long-term or short-term, has several advantages for the conductor and the ensemble. First of all, it calls for the clear stating of goals and provides a pathway to follow. As progress is made toward stated goals, the experience of closure takes place step by step as the choral sound matures. Finally, in performance, there is a clear-cut opportunity to measure musical growth and the process begins anew. In his book, LONG RANGE PLANNING, the author lists a series of stages in the planning process. Although the planning model is designed for large institutions, it is relevant to the context of this chapter and would allow the choral ensemble curriculum to serve as a microcosm of successful planning within a department of music in a secondary school. The order of planning is as follows: mission, goals, responsibilities, activities, budget and evaluation (PAREKH, Ch. 1). It follows that each is linked to the other from the time a philosophy of music education is established; the goals of the choral curriculum are defined; the responsibilities are delegated; the activities are planned and expedited; the budget is determined realistically in support of the activities; and finally, the musical results are measured in comparison with the original mission.

|

SUMMARY

In this chapter the authors have attempted to answer several specific questions that choral conductors face every day. The topics of communication with singers, the role of the conductor, interviewing and auditioning singers, vocalizing the ensemble, organizing rehearsal time, learning about changing voices, working with environmental factors, and planning ahead through assessment were presented sequentially, one leading to the other. The emphasis throughout the chapter has been on the changing role of the director, who must be teacher/conductor/planner as the need arises.

REFERENCES - Chapter 2

Abeles, Harold F.; Charles Hoffer and Robert Klotman. FOUNDATIONS OF MUSIC EDUCATION. Schirmer Books, Macmillan, Inc. New York, 1984.

Bessom, Malcolm E., Alphonse M. Tatarunis and Samuel L. Forcucci. TEACHING MUSIC IN TODAY'S SECONDARY SCHOOLS. Holt, Rinehart and Winston, New York, 1980.

Boyd, Jack. REHEARSAL GUIDE FOR THE CHORAL DIRECTOR. Parker Publishing Company, West Nyack, N.Y., 1970.

Cooksey, John. "The Development of a Contemporary, Eclectic Theory for the Training and Cultivation of the Junior High School Male Changing Voice, Part I, Existing Theories", THE CHORAL JOURNAL. Vol. XVIII, No. 2. October, 1977, Pp. 5-13.

Cooksey, John. "The Development of a Contemporary, Eclectic Theory for the Training and Cultivation of the Junior High School Male Changing Voice, Part II, Scientific and Empirical Findings: Some Tentative Solutions", THE CHORAL JOURNAL. Vol. XVIII, No. 3, November, 1977. Pp. 5-16.

Cooksey, John. "The Development of a Contemporary, Eclectic Theory for the Training and Cultivation of the Junior High School Male Changing Voice, Part III, Developing an Integrated Approach to the Care and Training of the Junior High School Male Changing Voice", THE CHORAL JOURNAL. Vol. XVIII, No. 4. December, 1977. Pp. 5-15.

Cooksey, John. "The Development of a Contemporary, Eclectic Theory for the Training and Cultivation of the Junior High School Male Changing Voice, Part IV, Selecting Music for the Junior High Male Changing Voice", THE CHORAL JOURNAL. Vol. XVIII, No. 5. January, 1978,

Cooper, Irvin and Karl O. Kuersteiner. TEACHING JUNIOR HIGH SCHOOL MUSIC, Allyn and Bacon, Boston, 1965.

Decker, Harold A. and Julius Herford (edit.). CHORAL CONDUCTING: A SYMPOSIUM. Prentice-Hall, Inc., Englewood Cliffs, N.J., 1973.

Ehmann, Wilhelm. CHORAL CONDUCTING, Augsburg Publishing House. Minneapolis, 1968.

Fenton, William C. "Choral Auditions: Content and Procedures", THE CHORAL JOURNAL. Vol. XXI, No. 7, March, 1981. Pp. 33-36.

Fenton, William C. "Improving Choral Sound Through Vocalization", THE CHORAL JOURNAL. Vol. XXIV, No. 2, October, 1978. Pp. 18-19.

Fenton, William C. "Music Education in the Coventry Cathedral: A Tribute to Tradition", TRIAD, Vol. XLVIII, No. 3, December, 1980. Pp. 14-15.

Finn, William J. THE ART OF THE CHORAL CONDUCTOR. (2nd edition). Summy-Birchard. Evanston, Illinois. 1960.

Furth, Hans G. PIAGET FOR TEACHERS. Prentice-Hall, Inc., Englewood Cliffs, N.J., 1970.

Geerdes, Harold. MUSIC BUILDINGS AND EQUIPMENT. Music Educators National Conference., Reston, Virginia.

Hammar, Russell. SINGING: AN EXTENSION OF SPEECH. The Scarecrow Press, Inc., London, 1978.

Heffernan, Charles W. CHORAL MUSIC: TECHNIQUE AND ARTISTRY. Prentice-Hall, Inc., Englewood Cliffs, N.J., 1982.

Holst, Imogen. CONDUCTING A CHOIR: A GUIDE FOR AMATEURS. Oxford University Press. London, 1973.

Howard, Francis E. THE CHILD-VOICE IN SINGING. Novello and Company, Ltd., London, 1923.

Music Educators National Conference. THE SCHOOL MUSIC PROGRAM: DESCRIPTION AND STANDARDS. Second Edition. Reston, Virginia, 1986.

Parekh, Satish B. LONG RANGE PLANNING. Change Magazine Press., New Rochelle, N.Y., 1977.

Petersen, Anne C. "Those Gangly Years", PSYCHOLOGY TODAY. Vol. XXI, No. 9, September, 1987. Pp. 28-34.

Roe, Paul F. CHORAL MUSIC EDUCATION. Prentice-Hall, Inc., Englewood Cliffs, N.J. 1970.

Singleton, Ira C. and Simon V. Anderson. MUSIC IN SECONDARY SCHOOLS. Allyn and Bacon, Inc., Boston, 1969.

Swanson, Frederick J. MUSIC TEACHING IN THE JUNIOR HIGH AND MIDDLE SCHOOL. Prentice-Hall, Inc., Englewood Cliffs, N.J., 1973.

3. SINGING IN MULTIPLE LANGUAGES

Is it appropriate for junior and senior high school choirs to sing in foreign languages? Most directors would agree that rehearsal time is already limited. Will the teaching of pronunciation in a given language require a disproportionate amount of time for the value received? Does the director have the appropriate knowledge to undertake this task? How time consuming will preparation be?

The authors of this book maintain that it is appropriate to broaden the musical and cultural horizons of students by the singing of selected texts in their original languages. In a day when the study of foreign languages is receiving renewed emphasis in national studies on the quality of public education, the local school language program can be enhanced by the utilization of parallel languages in the choral music curriculum. The musical setting a composer prepares for a given text is carefully wedded to it through the rhythm, accent, stress of important words, appropriate intervalic movement, and careful growth of interpretative ideas. It is a rare translation that is able to accommodate all these factors. The United States is rich in the diversity of its people. Both from an historical prospective and the reality of present day heterogeneity, appreciation for the many cultures represented in this country can be furthered by the presentation of their music and languages.

The time necessary for the teaching of a foreign language text can be greatly reduced by the consistent use of the International Phonetic Alphabet, hereafter referred to as the I.P.A.. This tool, coupled with language pronunciation charts provided in this text in Italian, Latin, Spanish, Hebrew, German, and French should streamline the task at hand. Samples of songs transcribed into I.P.A. symbols for each language presented will provide a model for class presentation. A bibliography will provide access to more detailed information on each language.

THE INTERNATIONAL PHONETIC ALPHABET

The I.P.A. was originally devised in Europe in 1888 and has been revised periodically since that time. It consists of symbols representing each sound in a given language, regardless of its spelling. This system is international in scope because each symbol remains constant in every language that produces a given sound. Many of the symbols are identical to letters in the western alphabet. However, special care must be taken when using I.P.A. symbols, not to interchange upper and lower case letters, (ex. i and ɪ), or printed and written letters, (ex. a and ɑ). In both of these cases the I.P.A. symbols indicate different sounds. For example, [i] is the underlined sound in the word m<u>ee</u>t and would be written phonetically [mit]. [ɪ] is the sound underlined in the word t<u>i</u>p and would be written phonetically as [t ɪp]. Likewise, [a] indicates the underlined sound in the word c<u>a</u>t [kat] and [ɑ] indicates the sound in the word f<u>a</u>ther [fɑðr]. Notice the I.P.A. symbols are written in brackets [ ] whenever they might be confused with orthographic spellings.

The original spelling of words in a given language is considered its orthographic spelling, whereas the use of I.P.A. symbols to indicate the correct pronunciation of the word is referred to as the phonetic spelling. The complete phonetic spelling of a word, sentence, or complete text is called a phonetic transcription.

Appropriate I.P.A. symbols will be introduced in the discussion of each language to be presented. The format will be as follows, with additional columns provided for the orthographic and phonetic spellings of the language being presented.

I.P.A. Symbols	Orthographic English Spelling	Phonetic English Transcription
ɛ	g<u>e</u>t	gɛt
ʤ	<u>j</u>et	ʤɛt

The speed with which any new language can be pronounced is greatly increased as students acquire a 'vocabulary' of I.P.A. symbols. Although orthographic spellings may vary from language to language, the I.P.A. symbols will teach the correct sound as the following underlined examples will illustrate. The symbol [ʃ] will have different orthographic spellings but the same sound in the languages illustrated below.

I.P.A. Symbol	Orthographic English Spelling	Orthographic Italian Spelling	Orthographic German Spelling	Orthographic French Spelling
ʃ	<u>sh</u>oe	pe<u>sc</u>i	<u>s</u>prechen	mou<u>ch</u>oir

Orthographic Hebrew Spelling	Orthographic Spanish Spelling
<u>sh</u>abbat	does not exist

ITALIAN - THE SINGER'S LANGUAGE

There are numerous benefits that a choral ensemble can realize from the singing of Italian. The following language characteristics will not only help development of choral blend, precise diction and desireable tone quality for the ensemble, but will contribute to the vocal development of individual singers.

Italian is a relatively easy language to pronounce with only seven vowel sounds as compared to more than fifteen in English. The openness of the language can be attributed to at least two characteristics. First of all, Italian consonants that involve the tip of the tongue are pronounced with the tongue touching the upper teeth, not at the gum ridge as in English. The result of the lower tongue position is that there is more space in the mouth above the tongue. Secondly, many single vowels in English function as diphthongs. They have two vowel sounds that are pronounced so that the second vowel brings the mouth to a more closed position. Couple this with the fact that most words in English end with a consonant and we find that English speech habits work against an open "let go" use of the mouth and throat in singing. Italian, on the other hand has no single vowels that function as diphthongs and has very few words that do not end in a vowel.

A comfortably open mouth position should be learned early in singing if full resonance and freedom are to be achieved. Singing in Italian helps to achieve this desired openness, but only if students learn to sing Italian without the closures inherent in English. Italian, pronounced correctly, will teach valuable lessons in minimizing the closures in singing English and other languages. It follows then, that vocalising with Italian syllables will help achieve this goal (see chapters 1 & 2).

Now let us turn our attention to the Italian Pronunciation and I.P.A Symbols Chart. Notice that columns are presented that show the orthographic spelling of a given sound followed by a column showing the appropriate symbol for that sound. Subsequent columns then illustrate the approximate sound in an English word and then an Italian word which is written both orthographically and phonetically. In each case, the specific sound being illustrated is underlined. This chart is followed by a section on general rules of Italian Pronunciation. A dictionary should be consulted as needed to determine pronunciation of "e" and "o".

ITALIAN PRONUNCIATION & IPA SYMBOLS CHART

Orthographic Italian Letters	Phonetic Symbol	Orthographic English Spelling	Orthographic Italian Spelling	Phonetic Italian Transcription
Vowels				
i	i	f<u>ee</u>t	m<u>i</u>	[mi̠]
e (closed)	e	ch<u>ao</u>s	m<u>e</u>	[me̠]
e (open)	ɛ	m<u>e</u>t	b<u>e</u>n	[bɛn]
o (closed)	o	<u>o</u>mit	d<u>o</u>mani	[do̠mɑni]
o (open)	ɔ	<u>o</u>rphan	c<u>o</u>re	[kɔre]
a	ɑ	f<u>a</u>ther	c<u>a</u>ro	[kɑro]
u	u	p<u>oo</u>l	p<u>u</u>r	[pu̠r]
Semi - Vowels				
i	j	<u>y</u>ou	p<u>i</u>u	[pi̠u]
u	w	s<u>u</u>ave	q<u>u</u>ando	[kwɑndo]
Consonants				
b	b	<u>b</u>oat	<u>b</u>ene	[b̠ene]
c (before a,o,u or any consonant)	k	<u>c</u>ar	<u>c</u>aro	[k̠ɑro]
ch	k	<u>k</u>art	<u>ch</u>e	[k̠e]
c (before i,e)	tʃ	<u>c</u>ello	<u>c</u>erca	[tʃerkɑ]
d	d	<u>d</u>og	<u>d</u>anza	[d̠ɑntsɑ]
f	f	<u>f</u>or	<u>f</u>orte	[fɔrte]
g (before a,o,u or any consonant except l or n)	g	<u>g</u>ive	<u>g</u>amba	[gɑmbɑ]
g (before h)	g	<u>g</u>ive	<u>gh</u>irlanda	[g̠irlɑndɑ]
g (before i,e)	ʤ	<u>g</u>entle	<u>g</u>entile	[ʤɛntile]
gli	ʎ	(similar to) ha<u>lli</u>ard	fi<u>gli</u>a	[fiʎɑ]
h	not sounded			
l	l	<u>l</u>ove	<u>l</u>ungo	[l̠uŋgo]
m	m	<u>m</u>other	<u>m</u>adre	[m̠ɑdre]
n	n	<u>n</u>o	<u>n</u>on	[n̠on]
(g)n	ɲ	(similar to) o<u>ni</u>on	o<u>gni</u>	[oɲi]
n(g followed by a,o,u)	ŋ	sa<u>ng</u>	a<u>ng</u>olo	[ɑŋɔlo]
p	p	<u>p</u>our	<u>p</u>adre	[p̠ɑdre]
q	k	<u>q</u>uick	<u>q</u>uando	[kwɑndo]
r (flipped or rolled)	r	<u>r</u>oll	<u>r</u>osa	[rɔzɑ]
s (voiced)	z	<u>z</u>eal	ro<u>s</u>a	[rɔ̠zɑ]

s (unvoiced)	s	<u>s</u>ee	<u>s</u>ento	[sɛnto]
sc (before i,e)	ʃ	<u>sh</u>ave	<u>sc</u>ena	[ʃɛnɑ]
sc (before a,o,u)	sk	<u>sc</u>out	<u>sc</u>ala	[skɑlɑ]
sci (before a,e,o,u)	ʃ	<u>sh</u>ave	la<u>sci</u>a	[lɑʃɑ]
t	t	<u>t</u>wo	tu<u>tt</u>o	[tuʈʈo]
v	v	<u>v</u>ery	<u>v</u>erde	[vɛrde]
z , zz	ts	ge<u>ts</u>	<u>z</u>io	[tsio]
z , zz	dz	od<u>ds</u>	me<u>zz</u>o	[mɛdːzo]

General Guidelines for Italian Pronunciation

The following guidelines address only those spellings and sounds that require further explanation.

A. Accents (examples show accented or stressed syllables underlined.)

> **1. Most Italian words are accented on the penultimate syllable, but in singing the accented syllable of a word usually will be established by the musical line of a song.**
>
> Examples: Fed<u>e</u>le, c<u>e</u>rto, dol<u>o</u>re
>
> **2. When the final vowel of a word is stressed it is usually marked with a grave accent. This will also mean that "e" and "o" are usually pronounced [ɛ] and [ɔ]**
>
> Example: far<u>ò</u>, [fɑrɔ]
>
> **3. The grave accents can also determine different meanings of words spelled identically. For example, "di" means "of", while "dì" means "day". Here are some other examples of word meaning changed by the grave accent.**
>
> Examples: tè - tea, te - you
> è-he is, e-and
> sì-yes, si-himself

B. Vowels

1. Vowels are often described as being "open" or "close" (closed). The differences in sound directly relate to the open or close positions of the mouth as well as the position of the tongue as it effects the size of the oral cavity. The vowels "e" and "o" have two pronunciations in Italian and there is considerable disagreement as to when they are open and closed. Except in the situations described below, a dictionary should be used to determine their pronunciation.

    a. Final e and o are usually unaccented and are therefore pronounced closed.

    Examples: sempre   [sɛmpre]

                      caro   [karo]

    b. Final accented o is open.

    Examples: farò   [farɔ]

                      manderò   [mandɛrɔ]

2. The pronunciation of i.

    a. i is sounded as [i] in most instances

    Examples: vita   [vita]

                      si   [si]

    b. It is treated as a semi-vowel when unaccented and preceding another vowel.

    Examples: bianca   [bjaŋka]

                      piu   [pju]

    c. It is silent after gl when followed by a, e or o.

    Examples: figlio   [fiʎo]

                      veglia   [veʎa]

d. Before a, o and u it softens the sound of the preceding consonants and is usually not pronounced.

ci	[tʃ]	Example:	ciao	[tʃao]
gi	[dʒ]	Example:	gioio	[dʒɔjo]
sci	[ʃ]	Example:	lascia	[laʃa]

3. The vowel u is used in two ways.

a. It usually sounds as [u]

Examples: utile [utile]

  pur [pur]

b. It is treated as a semi-vowel when unaccented and preceding another vowel.

Examples: nuovo [nwɔvo]

  quella [kwɛlla]

4. Unstressed vowels must not be slighted as is often done in English.

Examples: general [dʒɛnrl] English

  generale [dʒɛnralɛ] Italian

5. Single Italian vowels are not diphthongized. (see page 97)

6. When the final vowel of a word is tied to a different vowel of the second word and is sung on a single note a textual diphthong exists. Equal time should be given to the two vowels.

Examples: che un [ke un]

  se il [se il]

If the same vowel is repeated it elides.

Examples: mite e [mite]

  lamassi indaro [lamassi indaro]

C. Consonants

1. **d, t, l, n** and **r** are dental consonants and are pronounced with the tip of the tongue placed on the upper teeth instead of on the gum ridge as in English.

2. **r** is flipped when it is single between two vowels in the same word or final in a word preceding a word beginning with a vowel.

Examples: core   [kɔre]
           amor amor   [amor amor]

Most other r's are rolled. Practice flipping r's by pronouncing words that begin with **dr**, such as drink, droop, etc. Once this is mastered, add more breath pressure and sustain into a roll.

3. **h** is silent but indicates the hard sound of c or g before i and e.

Examples: che   [ke]
           ghiro   [giro]

4. **s** has two sounds.

a. Voiced (with phonation) [dz]

(1) It is always voiced before the voiced consonants **b, d, g, l, m, n, r, v.**

Examples: sdegno   [zdeɲo]
           sventura   [zventura]

(2) Between vowels it should be voiced almost exclusively in singing, even if unvoiced in speech.

Examples: rosa   [roza]
           casa   [kaza]

b. Unvoiced (without phonation) [s]

In all other instances.

Examples: sento   [sɛnto]
           cassa   [kassa]

5. z has two sounds,

The best rule to determine which pronunciation is appropriate is to consult a good Italian dictionary.

a. Voiced [dz]

Examples: bonzo   [bondːzo]
            mezzo   [mɛdːzo]

b. Unvoiced [ts]

Examples: grazie   [gratsjɛ]
            silenzio [silɛntsjo]

6. j, k, w, x and y are not considered part of the modern Italian alphabet and are only found in old song texts or in words adopted from another language. Use the dictionary for their pronunciation.

D. Doubled Consonants

Doubled consonants in Italian require special attention. They must be treated differently than their single counterparts or word meaning may be altered. For example, bela - [bela] translates as 'it bleats' whereas bella - [bɛlla] means 'beautiful'.

1. Treatment of doubled consonants is determined by the production of that consonant. Those letters that have a continuing sound are doubled in length. They are ff, mm, nn, ll, rr, ss and vv. They are transcribed as follows.

Examples: mamma   [mamma]
            messa   [mɛssa]

The doubled I.P.A. symbol shows the elongation of the sound.

2. The doubled consonants bb, cc, dd, gg, pp, tt and zz are given a different treatment. The breath is stopped momentarily between consonants and allowed to explode, (thereby given the name 'plosive') only on the second consonant. Here are some examples of this kind of delayed plosive sound in English. Please note the underlined letters. The ː indicates the delayed plosive sound.

Bob boat	talk candidly	Hatchet	dead dog
loud jet	log garage	stop Pat	get tough
pretzel	add zero		

Now for some examples in Italian, with added phonetic transcriptions of each word.

babbo	[bab:bo]	tocca	[tɔk:ka]	faccia	[fat:ʃa]
freddo	[fred:do]	laggiu	[ladʒu]	stappi	[stap:pi]
tutto	[tut:to]	pizza	[pitsa]	mezzo	[mɛd:zo]

"Bella vita militar" from Così Fan Tutte
[bɛlla vita militar]   [kozi fɑn tut:te]

libretto by Lorenzo Da Ponte

Bella vita militar,
    [bɛlla vita militar

Ogni di si cangia loco
    oɲi di si kandʒja loko

oggi molto, doman poco,
    ɔdʒi mɔlto doman poko

ora in terra ed or sul mar.
    ora in tɛrra ɛd ɔr sul mar

Il frago di trombe e pifferi'
    il frago di trɔmbe e pifɛri

lo sparar di schioppi e bombe
    lo sparar di skjɔp:pi e bɔmbe

forza accresce al braccio,
    fɔrtsa ak:kreʃe al brat:ʃjo

e all' anima vaga sol di trionfar.
    e all anima vaga sɔl di trjɔnfar

Bella vita militar!
    bɛlla vita militar]

104

LITURGICAL LATIN

Liturgical Latin (i.e. Ecclesiastical or Church Latin) is an important language for junior and senior high choral groups. Next to English, it will be the most commonly sung language for these ensembles. Care should be taken not to confuse Liturgical Latin with the Classical Latin used in high school Latin courses. Their origins differ, and it follows there are pronunciation differences.

The following Liturgical Latin Chart shows the strong similarities between the Italian and Latin Languages. The General Guidelines will specifically point out pronunciation differences between the two languages.

LATIN PRONUNCIATION & IPA SYMBOLS CHART

Orthographic Latin Letters	Phonetic Symbol	Orthographic English Spelling	Orthographic Latin Spelling	Phonetic Latin Transcription
Vowels				
i	i	f<u>ee</u>t	nob<u>i</u>s	[nɔb<u>i</u>s]
e	ɛ	m<u>e</u>t	s<u>e</u>dit	[s<u>ɛ</u>dit]
ae	ɛ	m<u>e</u>t	s<u>ae</u>cula	[s<u>ɛ</u>kulɑ]
oe	ɛ	m<u>e</u>t	c<u>oe</u>li	[tʃ<u>ɛ</u>li]
o	ɔ	<u>o</u>rphan	t<u>o</u>tum	[t<u>ɔ</u>tum]
a	ɑ	f<u>a</u>ther	tu<u>a</u>	[tu<u>ɑ</u>]
u	u	p<u>oo</u>l	fact<u>u</u>m	[fɑkt<u>u</u>m]
y	i	s<u>ee</u>	K<u>y</u>rie	[k<u>i</u>riɛ]
Consonants				
b	b	<u>b</u>oat	<u>b</u>onae	[<u>b</u>ɔnɛ]
c (before a,o,u)	k	<u>c</u>ar	<u>c</u>um	[<u>k</u>um]
ch	k	<u>k</u>art	<u>Ch</u>ristus	[<u>k</u>ristus]
c (before i,e,oe,ae)	tʃ	<u>c</u>ello	pa<u>c</u>em	[pɑ<u>tʃ</u>ɛm]
d	d	<u>d</u>og	a<u>d</u>	[ɑ<u>d</u>]
f	f	<u>f</u>or	<u>f</u>ili	[<u>f</u>ili]
g (before a,o.u or consonant)	ɡ	<u>g</u>ive	vir<u>g</u>o	[vir<u>ɡ</u>ɔ]
*h	silent			
l	l	<u>l</u>ove	<u>l</u>auda	[<u>l</u>ɑudɑ]
m	m	<u>m</u>ine	<u>M</u>aria	[<u>m</u>ɑriɑ]

n	n	<u>n</u>o	<u>n</u>obis	[<u>n</u>ɔbis]
gn	ɲ	o<u>ni</u>on	a<u>gn</u>us	[a<u>ɲ</u>us]
p	p	<u>p</u>our	<u>p</u>ropter	[<u>p</u>rɔptɛr]
q	k	<u>q</u>uick	<u>q</u>ui	[<u>k</u>wi]
r	r	<u>r</u>oll	<u>R</u>ex	[<u>r</u>ɛks]
s (between vowels)	z	Je<u>s</u>us	Je<u>s</u>u	[jɛ<u>z</u>u]
s	s	<u>s</u>ee	<u>s</u>ede<u>s</u>	[<u>s</u>ɛdɛ<u>s</u>]
sc (before i,e,ae,oe)	ʃ	<u>sh</u>ave	su<u>sc</u>ipe	[suʃipɛ]
sc (before a,o,u consonants)	sk	<u>sc</u>our	vobi<u>sc</u>um	[vɔbi<u>sk</u>um]
t	t	<u>t</u>wo	<u>t</u>ibi	[<u>t</u>ibi]
v	v	<u>v</u>ery	<u>v</u>eritas	[<u>v</u>ɛritɑs]
x (before vowels or h)	gz	e<u>gg</u>s	e<u>x</u>audi	[ɛ<u>gz</u>ɑudi]
x	ks	e<u>x</u>tra	lu<u>x</u>	[lu<u>ks</u>]
z	dz	o<u>dd</u>s	la<u>z</u>aro	[lɑ<u>dz</u>arɔ]

* exceptions - consult dictionary

General Guidelines to Liturgical Latin Pronunciation

Liturgical Latin follows the same pronunciation rules that apply to Italian with the following exceptions. [ ] indicates I.P.A. symbols.

A. Stress - Accents

Stress in Latin is not as strong as it is in Italian. It will usually fall on the penultimate or antepenultimate syllable.

B. Vowels

1. Orthographic e and o are always open in Liturgical Latin.

Examples: r<u>e</u>qui<u>e</u>m [r<u>ɛ</u>kwi<u>ɛ</u>m]
 D<u>o</u>minus [d<u>ɔ</u>minus]

2. The vowel combinations ae and oe are pronounced [ɛ].

They are treated as orthographic e when determining the pronunciation of c and g.

Examples: ir<u>ae</u>   [irɛ]

coelum   [tʃɛlum]

3. The dieresis (") over the second vowel in the above combinations indicates the separate sounding of each vowel.

Example: Raphaël   [rɑfɑɛl]

4. All other consecutive vowels are pronounced separately.

C. Consonants

1. H is silent except in the words Mihi and nihil, which were originally spelled michi and nichil. These words are pronounced [miçi] and [niçil].

2. j is pronounced [j].

Examples: Jesu   [jɛzu]

justi   [justi]

3. r is lightly flipped

Examples: gloria   [glɔria]

Christus   [kristus]

4. ti is pronounced as [tsi] when preceding a vowel.

Examples: gratia   [grɑtsiɑ]

ultionis   [ultsiɔnis]

5. Th is pronounced [t]

Example: throni   [trɔni]
         Catholicam   [katɔlikɑm]

6. x has several pronunciations.

a. It sounds as [gz] in initial syllables when it is preceded by an e and followed by another vowel or h.

Examples: exaudi   [ɛgzɑudi]
            exhibeo   [ɛgzibɛɔ]

b. When xc is followed by e, i, y, ae, or oe the combined sound is transcribed as [ɛkʃ]

Examples: excelsis   [ɛkʃɛlsis]
            excessus   [ɛkʃɛssus]

c. In all other cases it sounds as [ks].

Examples: lux   [luks]
            pax   [pɑks]

7. z is pronounced [dz]

Example: Lazarus   [lɑdzɑrɔ]

REQUIEM AETERNAM, KYRIE
[rɛkwiɛm ɛtɛrnam kiriɛ]
Roman Catholic Liturgy

Requiem aeternam dona eis, Domine:
  [rɛkwiɛm ɛtɛrnam dɔna ɛis dɔminɛ

et lux perpetua luceat eis.
  ɛt luks pɛrpɛtua lutʃɛat ɛis

Te decet hymnus Deus in Sion,
  tɛ dɛtʃɛt imnus dɛus in siɔn

et tibi reddetur votum in Jerusalem:
  ɛt tibi rɛdɛtur vɔtum in jɛruzalɛm

exaudi orationem meam,
  ɛgzaudi ɔratsiɔnɛm mɛam

ad te omnis caro veniet.
  ad tɛ ɔmnis karɔ vɛniɛt

Requiem
  rɛkwiɛm

Kyrie eleison, Christe, eleison, Kyrie eleison
  kiriɛ ɛlɛizɔn kristɛ ɛlɛizɔn kiriɛ ɛlɛizɔn

Requiem aeternam dona eis Domine:
  rɛkwiɛm ɛtɛrnam dɔna ɛis dɔminɛ

et lux perpetua luceat eis.
  ɛt luks pɛrpɛtua lutʃɛat ɛis

In memoria aeterna erit justus:
  in mɛmɔria ɛtɛɪna ɛrit justus

ab auditione mala non timebit.
  ab auditsiɔnɛ mala nɔn timɛbit]

SPANISH

The United States has strong Spanish influence in its history. The last decade has seen a large increase in the Hispanic population of our country as immigration from Cuba, Mexico and other Latin and South American countries has grown. Certainly the music from the Hispanic countries should have a place in the choral curriculum of our schools.

In presenting the pronunciation of the Spanish language we confine the discussion to Castillian Spanish and Latin American - Mexican Spanish. This will give a good basis for acceptable pronunciation of most choral music in Spanish. However, the choral director should be aware of the fact that many different Spanish dialects and regional differences do exist.

Castillian Spanish and Latin American - Mexican (hereafter referred to as LAM) Spanish differ in just a few instances. These will be indicated in the following chart. Spanish is very similar to Italian and Latin and so the foregoing discussions of those languages will aid your understanding of Spanish.

SPANISH PRONUNCIATION & I.P.A SYMBOLS CHART

Orthographic Spanish Letters	Phonetic Symbol	Orthographic English Spelling	Orthographic Spanish Spelling	Phonetic Spanish Transcription
Vowels				
i	i	s<u>ee</u>	s<u>i</u>	[si]
e	e	ch<u>a</u>os	qu<u>e</u>	[ke]
a	ɑ	f<u>a</u>ther	c<u>a</u>s<u>a</u>	[kɑsɑ]
o	o	r<u>o</u>se	r<u>o</u>sa	[rosɑ]
u	u	p<u>oo</u>l	t<u>u</u>	[tu]
y	i	bo<u>y</u>	ho<u>y</u>	[oi]
Semi-Vowels				
i (unaccented before a,e,o)	j	<u>y</u>ou	hac<u>i</u>a	[ɑθjɑ]
u (after c preceeding another vowel	w	q<u>u</u>ick	c<u>u</u>erda	[kwerðɑ]
u (before a,e,o)	w	q<u>u</u>ick	d<u>u</u>eño	[dweɲo]

Consonants

b (beginning consonant or preceding m,n)	b	a<u>b</u>olish (with little plosion)	<u>b</u>anca	[<u>b</u>aŋkɑ]
b (all others)	β	abo<u>v</u>e (lazy v)	ha<u>b</u>lar	[a<u>β</u>lar]
c (before a,o,u)	k	<u>c</u>ombine	<u>c</u>ombo	[kom<u>β</u>o]
c (before e,i) (Castillian)	θ	<u>th</u>in	<u>c</u>inco	[<u>θ</u>iŋko]
c (before e,i) (LAM)	s	<u>s</u>oon	<u>c</u>inco	[<u>s</u>iŋko]
cc (preceding i,e) (Castillian)	kθ	ba<u>ck th</u>in	a<u>cc</u>idente	[ak<u>θ</u>iðente]
cc (preceding i,e) (LAM)	ks	a<u>x</u>	a<u>cc</u>idente	[ak<u>s</u>iðente]
ch	ʧ	<u>ch</u>ew	no<u>ch</u>e	[noʧe]
d (initial or before m,n,l)	d	<u>d</u>og	<u>d</u>eseo	[<u>d</u>eseo]
d (middle of word)	ð	<u>th</u>ough	ale<u>d</u>año	[ale<u>ð</u>aɲo]
d (final)	ð	bo<u>th</u>	soleda<u>d</u>	[soleða<u>ð</u>]
f	f	<u>f</u>ind	<u>f</u>iera	[<u>f</u>jera]
g (before a consonant and preceding a,o,u when initial in a breath group, or after n)	g	<u>g</u>o	<u>g</u>ato	[<u>g</u>ato]
g (preceding a,o within a breath group)	x	Ba<u>ch</u>	la<u>g</u>o	[la<u>x</u>o]
g (preceding i,e)	ç	<u>h</u>uman	<u>g</u>entil	[<u>ç</u>entil]
gu (before e,i)	g	<u>gu</u>ess	<u>gu</u>iso	[<u>g</u>iso]
gu (before a,o)	gw	<u>Gw</u>en	<u>gu</u>arda	[<u>gw</u>arda]
h	silent			
j	ç	<u>h</u>uman	<u>j</u>ota	[<u>ç</u>ota]
l	l	<u>l</u>ove	<u>l</u>as	[<u>l</u>as]
ll (Castillian)	ʎ	bri<u>ll</u>iant	<u>ll</u>orar	[<u>ʎ</u>orar]
ll (Some LAM)	j	<u>y</u>es	<u>ll</u>orar	[<u>j</u>orar]
m	m	<u>m</u>ove	<u>m</u>esa	[<u>m</u>esa]
n	n	<u>n</u>ow	<u>n</u>oche	[<u>n</u>oʧe]
n (before b,v,p)	m	<u>m</u>arry	e<u>n</u>vidia	[e<u>m</u>βiðja]
n (before [g] or [k])	ŋ	u<u>n</u>cle	sa<u>n</u>gre	[sa<u>ŋ</u>gre]
ñ	ɲ	can<u>y</u>on	pi<u>ñ</u>a	[pi<u>ɲ</u>a]
p	p (with little plosion)	<u>p</u>oor	<u>p</u>ero	[<u>p</u>ero]

qu	k	<u>k</u>ind	por<u>qu</u>e	[por<u>k</u>e]
r (initial and rr)	r (rolled)	—	<u>r</u>ico	[<u>r̠</u>iko]
r (within a word)	r (flipped)	t<u>r</u>ip	co<u>r</u>o	[ko<u>r̠</u>o]
s	s	<u>s</u>ing	<u>s</u>obar	[so<u>β</u>ɑr]
s (before voiced consonants)	z	<u>z</u>ero	ra<u>s</u>gar	[ra<u>z</u>gɑr]
t	t	<u>t</u>oday	<u>t</u>res	[<u>t</u>res]
v	β	lo<u>v</u>e	<u>v</u>erde	[<u>β</u>erðe]
		(lazy v with lips close together)		
y	j	<u>y</u>es	<u>y</u>o	[<u>j</u>o]
x	ks	ki<u>ck</u>s	e<u>x</u>amine	[ɛ<u>ks</u>amine]
x	ç (some LAM)	<u>h</u>uman	Me<u>x</u>ico	[me<u>ç</u>iko]
z	θ (Castillian)	<u>th</u>in	cora<u>z</u>on	[korɑ<u>θ</u>on]
z	s (LAM)	<u>s</u>on	cora<u>z</u>on	[korɑ<u>s</u>on]

General Guidelines to Spanish Pronunciation

The following guidelines address only those spellings and sounds which require further explanation.

A. Stress-Accents

1. Words ending in a vowel, or in n or s, are stressed on the penultimate syllable.

Examples: <u>p</u>adre, <u>ha</u>blan, <u>ca</u>mpos

2. Words ending in a consonant other than n or s are accented on the last syllable.

Examples: sole<u>dad</u>, habl<u>ar</u>, jal<u>ar</u>

3. Exceptions to rule 1 and 2 will indicate stress by placing an accent mark (´) over the vowel to be stressed.

Examples: <u>có</u>nsul, telé<u>f</u>ono, caf<u>é</u>

4. The acute accent mark (´) is also used to distinguish between homonyms.

Examples: el - the, él - he
este - this, éste - this one

B. Vowels

1. Spanish vowels are closed.

2. i and u become semi-consonants [j, w] when preceding other vowels.

Examples: hac̲i̲a   [aθja]
c̲u̲andro   [kwanðro]

3. u is always silent when it follows g or q and is in turn followed by i, e.

Examples: g̲u̲i   [gi]
q̲u̲e   [ke]

4. In the above situation (3) the dieresis (") over the u will restore its sound.

Examples: agüelo   [agwelo]
güero   [gwero]

5. y can be treated as a vowel [i] or a consonant [j].

Examples: ho̲y̲   [oi̯]
y̲o   [jo]

C. Consonants

1. Double consonants are doubly sounded.

Examples: co̲r̲ro   [korro]
deduc̲c̲ión   [dedukθion]

2. r is rolled when it is the initial sound or is doubled.

Examples: rico   [r̠iko]
          garra   [gɑr̠ɑ]

It is flipped in other instances.

Examples: llorar   [ʎor̠ɑr̠]
          herido [er̠iðo]

See page 102 under Italian r for drills to perfect rolled or flipped r.

3. Final d is very weak.

Examples: soledad   [soleðɑḏ]
          Madrid   [mɑðriḏ]

PASTORES A BELEN
[pastores a belen]

A Spanish Carol
(Castillian Spanish)

Pastores a Belen, vamos con alegria,
   [pastores a belen βamos kon alegria

A ver a nuestro bien, al hijo de Maria
   a βer a nwestro bjen al iço de maria

Alli, alli, alli nos espera Jesus!
   ali ali ali nos espera çesus

Entrad, entrad, pastores,
      entraɗ   entraɗ   pastores

Entrad, entrad, zagalas tambien.
      entraɗ entraɗ θagalas tamβjen

Vamos a ver al recien nacido,
      βamos a βer al reθjen naθiðo

Vamos a ver al Niño Manuel.
      βamos a βer al niɲo manwel]

CHIAPANECAS
[ʧjapanekas]

Mexican Folk Dance and Song
LAM

Soy de Chiapas, Tierra linda, Donde todas las mujeres,
  [soi de ʧjapas tjerra linða donðe toðaz laz muçeres

Son valientes, y bonitas, y buenas palos quereres,
  son βaljentes i bonitas i bwenas palos kereres

Soy de Chiapas, Tierra linda, Donde todas las mujeres,
  soi de ʧjapas tjerra linða donðe toðaz laz muçeres

Son valientes, y bonitas, y buenas palos quereres,
  son βaljentes i bonitas i bwenas palos kereres

Y si un mocito se a cerca a mi, y muy queditame dice, ah si,
  i si un mosito se a serka a mi i mui keðitame dise a si

Ay chiapa linda por tu querer, Daria la vida y el corazon.
  ai ʧjapa linða por tu kerer darja la βiða i el korason

!Ay! !Ay! linda muchacha, !Ay! !Ay! linda muchacha, !Ay! !Ay!
Olé!
  ai ai linða muʧaʧa ai ai linða muʧaʧa ai ai ole]

HEBREW

Most singers will approach Hebrew as a transliteration, i.e. a phonetic representation of the Hebrew characters, using our Roman alphabet. This process is often referred to as Romanization. Confusion sometimes arises because transliterators of varying nationalities transcribe the Hebrew texts using the orthographic spellings of their native language. As a result, transcriptions by a Frenchman and a German could have considerably different spellings. The nationality of the transliterator usually is obvious from the transliteration, thereby determining which language's rules of pronunciation to follow.

There are many regional differences in Hebrew but the most common dialects are Sephardi and Ashkenazi. Sephardi has been adopted by Israel and most universities throughout the world because it is believed to be nearest the original pronunciation of Hebrew. It is not unusual to find older music publications using Ashkenazi instead of Sephardi. The basic differences are as folows.

Ashkenasi	Sephardi
oi [ɔi] changes to	ai [ɑi]
o [ɔ] sometimes changes to	a [ɑ]
s [s] sometimes changes to	t [t]

Not all orthographic spellings of the above sounds change between Ashkenazi and Sephardi. Although these complexities may require additional research on the part of the choral director, (most probably consultation with a local Rabbi or Cantor), the effort required will be rewarded by access to interesting folk songs and inspiring religious selections.

The following chart and guidelines are based on Sephardi Hebrew.

HEBREW PRONUNCIATION & I.P.A. SYMBOLS CHART

Orthographic Hebrew Letters	Phonetic Symbol	Orthographic English Spelling	Orthographic Hebrew Spelling	Phonetic Hebrew Transcription
Vowels				
a	ɑ	f<u>a</u>ther	m<u>a</u>lchay	[m<u>ɑ</u>lxei]
ay	ei	m<u>ay</u>	hal<u>ay</u>la	[hal<u>ei</u>la
ai	ai	b<u>y</u>	adon<u>ai</u>	[adon<u>ai</u>]
e (in stressed final syllables)	e	ch<u>a</u>os	hanev<u>e</u>l	[hanɛv<u>e</u>l]
e (usually)	ɛ	g<u>e</u>t	alaych<u>e</u>m	[al<u>e</u>ixɛm]
ee	i	s<u>ee</u>	hamloch<u>ee</u>m	[hamlox<u>i</u>m]
ei	ei	m<u>ay</u>	al<u>ei</u>chem	[al<u>ei</u>xɛm]
ey	ei	m<u>ay</u>	eloh<u>ey</u>nu	[ɛloh<u>ei</u>nu]
i	i	s<u>ee</u>	nag<u>i</u>la	[nag<u>i</u>la]
o	o	g<u>o</u>ats	ad<u>o</u>nai	[ad<u>o</u>nai]
u	u	p<u>oo</u>l	v'sham'r<u>u</u>	[veʃamər<u>u</u>]
raised e or ' (separation vowel)	ə	th<u>e</u>	v<u>e</u>sham'ru	[v<u>ə</u>ʃaməru]
Consonants				
b	b	<u>b</u>oy	<u>b</u>arᵉchu	[<u>b</u>arəxu]
ch	x	Ba<u>ch</u>	barᵉ<u>ch</u>u	[barə<u>x</u>u]
d	d	<u>d</u>one	vae<u>d</u>	[vae<u>d</u>]
f	f	so<u>f</u>a	sho<u>f</u>ar	[ʃo<u>f</u>ar]
g	g	<u>g</u>one	<u>g</u>adal	[<u>g</u>adal]
h	h	<u>h</u>ave	<u>h</u>ashalom	[<u>h</u>aʃalom]
h	silent after a vowel when final		ze<u>h</u>	[zɛ<u>h</u>]
k	k	<u>k</u>ing	<u>k</u>i	[<u>k</u>i]
l	l	<u>l</u>ive	nagi<u>l</u>a	[nagi<u>l</u>a]
m	m	<u>m</u>en	shala<u>m</u>	[ʃala<u>m</u>]
n	n	<u>n</u>ow	<u>n</u>agila	[<u>n</u>agila]
p	p	<u>p</u>ush	<u>p</u>e	[<u>p</u>e]
r	r	t<u>r</u>ay	v'shom'<u>r</u>u	[vəʃamə<u>r</u>u]
	(flipped)			
s	s	<u>s</u>ay	Yi<u>s</u>rael	[ji<u>s</u>raɛl]
sh	ʃ	<u>sh</u>e	<u>sh</u>'ma	[<u>ʃ</u>əma]
t	t	<u>t</u>op	ha<u>t</u>ikvah	[ha<u>t</u>ikva]
th (final)	t	be<u>t</u>	Be<u>th</u>	[bɛ<u>t</u>]
v	v	<u>v</u>ery	<u>v</u>'sham'ru	[<u>v</u>əʃaməru]
y (when a consonant)	j	<u>y</u>ear	<u>Y</u>israel	[<u>j</u>ısraɛl]
z	z	<u>z</u>ero	<u>z</u>um	[<u>z</u>um]
z (following t)	s	bite<u>s</u>	aret<u>z</u>	[arɛt<u>s</u>]

General Guidelines to Hebrew Pronunciation

The following guidelines address only those spellings and sounds which require further explanation.

A. Vowels

1. Vowels in combination are given equal stress.

Example: Yisra̲e̲l   [jIsrɑɛl]

3. Separation vowels are indicated by a small raised letter (ᵉ) or an apostrophe ('). They are pronounced as a schwa [ə]. If no note is provided for this syllable, it is silent.

Example: v'ney   [və̠nci]
            vᵉshom'ru   [vəʃɑmɔru]

B. Consonants

1. The flipped r is usually used in Hebrew. See the section on Italian Pronunciation for suggestions to produce this sound.

2. ch, pronounced [x] as in Ba<u>ch</u> is produced by bringing the back of the tongue close to the soft palate and exhaling forcefully (as in German).

Examples: b'ru<u>ch</u> [bɔru<u>x</u>]
            eile<u>ch</u> [cilɛ<u>x</u>]

AVINU MALKENU
[ɑvinu mɑlkenu]

Liturgical Hebrew Text

Avinu malkenu sh'makolenu, Avinu malkenu chatanu l'fanecha
[ɑvinu mɑlkenu ʃəmakolenu ɑvinu mɑlkenu xɑtɑnu ləfanɛxɑ

Avinu malkenu chamol alenu v'al alolenu v'tapenu.
 ɑvinu mɑlkenu xɑmol ɑlenu vəɑl ɑlolenu vətɑpenu

Avinu malkenu kale dever v'cherev v'raav mealenu,
 ɑvinu mɑlkenu kɑle dɛvɛr vəxɛrev vəraɑv mealɛnu

Avinu malkenu kale chal tsar umastin mealenu.
 ɑvinu mɑlkenu kɑle xɑl tsɑr umɑstin mealenu

Avinu malkenu katvenu b'sefer chayim tovim,
 ɑvinu mɑlkenu kɑtvenu bəsefɛr xɑjim tovim

Avinu malkenu chadesh alenu, chadesh alenu shana tova.
 ɑvinu mɑlkenu xɑdɛʃ ɑlenu xɑdɛʃ ɑlenu ʃɑnɑ tɔvɑ

Avinu malkenu sh'ma kolenu, sh'ma kalenu.
 ɑvinu mɑlkenu ʃəmɑ kolenu ʃəmɑ kolenu

GERMAN

Fortunately, there are many fine translations of choral literature in German, the language of the three great B's—Bach, Beethoven and Brahms. The list of outstanding German and Austrian choral composers to be sampled is endless. Although translations are readily available for much of this literature, the advantages of singing in the original language deserve strong consideration. As mentioned early in this chapter, the composer carefully designs his music to compliment the text through melodic and rhythmic development. In translation, as word order and language characteristics change, some of the composer's or poet's original intentions must be compromised.

The German language almost seems familiar to us as we first approach it, for there are many cognates in English and German. That is, there are many words that look alike or sound similar. This is a mixed blessing as the tendency is to pronounce the word as is appropriate in your mother tongue (presumably English), rather than in the lesser known language. For instance, 'hand' in English [hand] equals [hɑnt] in German, or 'quick' in English [kwɪk] will be [kvɪkə] in German.

German is a very consonant language, with back consonants which some people consider gutteral. ch in Ba<u>ch</u> [bɑx] or in <u>ich</u> [iç] are sounds that will require special care and drill. The glottal stroke indicated by ʔ before an initial vowel such as e in ewig [ɛwɪç] is typical of the language, but should be used judiciously as it can be hard on untrained voices. As you can see, there is a challenge to be true to language characteristics when singing a legato line. Another challenge is the perfection of umlaut sounds such as ö in schön [ʃøn] or ü in Müller [mylləɾ]. The formation of all these sounds will be discussed in detail in the section General Guidelines to German Pronunciation.

The following pronunciation chart is based in Die Bühnenaussprache or stage German and will not always be consistent with idiomatic conversational German. Vowels in German can be either open or closed and also can vary in time duration. Anytime there are alternate sounds for a spelling, a dictionary should be consulted.

GERMAN PRONUNCIATION & I.P.A. SYMBOLS CHART

Orthographic German Letters	Phonetic Symbol	Orthographic English Spelling	Orthographic German Spelling	Phonetic German Transcription
Vowels				
a,ah	ɑ	f<u>a</u>ther	K<u>a</u>hn	[kɑn]
e,ee,eh	e	ch<u>ao</u>s	T<u>ee</u>r	[t<u>e</u>r]
e	ɛ	g<u>e</u>t	w<u>e</u>g	[v<u>ɛ</u>k]
e (final,unstressed final syllables, some prefixes)	ə	quick<u>e</u>n	bad<u>e</u>n	[bɑdən]
i, ie, ih	i	bel<u>ie</u>ve	B<u>i</u>bel	[bibəl]
i	ɪ	<u>i</u>n	<u>i</u>n	[ɪn]
o,oo,oh	o	l<u>oa</u>n	R<u>o</u>se	[r<u>o</u>zə]
o	ɔ	<u>a</u>we	G<u>o</u>tt	[g<u>ɔ</u>t]
u,uh	u	f<u>oo</u>d	K<u>u</u>h	[ku]
u	ʊ	p<u>u</u>t	<u>u</u>nter	[ʊntər]
Umlauts				
ö, öh	ø	tongue [e] lips [o]	sch<u>ö</u>n	[ʃøn]
ö	œ	tongue [ɛ] lips [ɔ]	H<u>ö</u>lle	[hœlə]
ü, üh	y	tongue [i] lips [u]	L<u>ü</u>ge	[lygə]
ü	Y	tongue [ɪ] lips [u]	f<u>ü</u>llen	[fɤlən]
ä, äh	ɛ	m<u>e</u>n	W<u>äh</u>ren	[vɛrən]
Vowel Combinations				
ai,ei	æ	m<u>i</u>ne	M<u>ei</u>n	[mɑen]
au	ɑo	h<u>ou</u>se	H<u>au</u>s	[hɑos]
ie	i	th<u>ie</u>ve	T<u>ie</u>f	t<u>i</u>f
eu, äu	ɔø	b<u>oy</u>	tr<u>eu</u>	[trɔø]
Consonants				
b	b	<u>b</u>ad	<u>B</u>ote	[botə]
b (end of word or syllable)	p	sto<u>p</u>	ha<u>b</u>	[hɑp]

c (before e,i,ä)	ts	hi<u>ts</u>	<u>c</u>is	[<u>ts</u>is]
ch (initial)	k	<u>k</u>ey	<u>Ch</u>or	[<u>k</u>or]
ch (following i,e)	ç	<u>h</u>uman	i<u>ch</u>	[ɪ<u>ç</u>]
ch (following a,o,u)	x	Ba<u>ch</u>	Ba<u>ch</u>	[bɑ<u>x</u>]
chs (occasionally doesn't follow rule)	ks	wa<u>x</u>	Se<u>chs</u>	[zɛ<u>ks</u>]
ck	k	Ki<u>ck</u>	Bli<u>ck</u>	[blɪ<u>k</u>]
c (all other times)	k	<u>k</u>ey	<u>C</u>reme	[<u>k</u>rɛmə]
d	d	<u>d</u>ine	<u>d</u>ein	[<u>d</u>aen]
d (final in word or syllable or in a final consonant cluster.)	t	<u>t</u>ime	Han<u>d</u>	[han<u>t</u>]
dt	t	<u>t</u>all	stä<u>dt</u>chen	[ʃtɛt<u>ç</u>ən]
f	f	<u>f</u>ine	<u>f</u>ein	[<u>f</u>aen]
g	g	<u>g</u>ive	<u>g</u>eben	[<u>g</u>ebən]
g (following i in final word or syllable)	ç	<u>h</u>uman	ewi<u>g</u>	[evɪ<u>ç</u>]
g (final in other words and syllables or in a final consonant cluster)	k	<u>k</u>ey	we<u>g</u>	[vɛ<u>k</u>]
(n) g	ŋ	ri<u>ng</u>	ri<u>ng</u>	[riŋ]
h	h	<u>h</u>ouse	<u>h</u>aus	[<u>h</u>aos]
h (after t)	silent		T<u>h</u>al	[tal]
j	j	<u>y</u>es	<u>j</u>a	[<u>j</u>a]
k	k	<u>k</u>ey	<u>K</u>opf	[<u>k</u>ɔpf]
l	l	<u>l</u>et	we<u>l</u>t	[vɛ<u>l</u>t]
m	m	<u>m</u>ine	<u>m</u>ein	[<u>m</u>aen]
n	n	<u>n</u>ine	<u>n</u>ein	[<u>n</u>aen]
n (before k in the same syllable)	ŋ	u<u>n</u>cle	sa<u>n</u>k	[zaŋk]
n (g) (in the same syllable)	ɲ	ri<u>ng</u>	ri<u>ng</u>	[riŋ]
p	p	<u>p</u>ast	<u>P</u>ost	[<u>p</u>ɔst]
pf	pf	cam<u>pf</u>ire	ko<u>pf</u>	[kɔ<u>pf</u>]
ph	f	<u>f</u>ine	<u>Ph</u>antast	[<u>f</u>antast]
qu	qv	ma<u>k</u>e <u>v</u>elvet	<u>qu</u>icke	[<u>kv</u>ɪk]
r (rolled or flipped)	r	t<u>r</u>eat	<u>r</u>eden	[<u>r</u>edən]
s (before vowel in the same syllable	z	<u>z</u>oo	<u>s</u>ehen	[<u>z</u>eən]
sch	ʃ	<u>s</u>ure	Fi<u>sch</u>en	[fɪ<u>ʃ</u>ən]
s (initial, followed by t,p)	ʃ	<u>s</u>ure	<u>s</u>pringen	[<u>ʃ</u>prɪŋən]

ss	s	mi**ss**	Wa**ss**er	[vɑsər]
t	t	**t**all	**T**ak**t**	[tɑkt]
th	t	**t**all	**Th**erme	[tɛrmə]
tz	ts	fi**ts**	si**tz**en	[zɪtsən]
v	f	**f**ine	**v**ater	[fɑtər]
w	v	**v**ery	**W**ein	[vɑen]
x	ks	**x**-ray	A**x**t	[ɑkst]
z	ts	i**ts**	**Z**eit	[tsɑet]

General Guidelines to German Pronunciation

The following guidelines address only those spellings and sounds which require further explanation.

A. Stress-Accents

1. Most German words are stressed on the first syllable.

Examples: <u>Va</u>ter

<u>Him</u>mel

2. Many words begin with prefixes which are inseparable, such as be, ent, ern ge, ver. These prefixes are never accented.

Examples: ent<u>deck</u>en

er<u>fah</u>ren

3. In words beginning with separable prefixes (prefixes that can stand alone as words), the prefix will be accented.

Examples: <u>ein</u>treten

<u>auf</u>geben

When there is confusion between inseparable and separable prefixes, consult a dictionary. This may also be necessary for rules 4, 5, and 6 which follow.

4. Words are frequently compounded in German. When this occurs, each component keeps its original stress, but the first component receives the strongest stress.

Examples: Hundehaus
Haushund

5. When the compound word is an adverb, stress usually falls on the second syllable.

Examples: zurück
hinaus

6. Stress is usually placed on the negative prefix un.

Examples: unverstanden
unwahr

7 The following common words are stressed on the second syllable, allein, warum, lebendig.

B. Vowels

Vowels in German can be either open or closed and also can vary in time duration therefore being long or short. Because time duration is really preset by musical notation in singing, the authors have chosen not to address the length of vowels. Likewise, some sources acknowledge two pronunciations of orthographic a. It is the authors' opinion that these sound differences, which may be significant in speech, become less significant when lengthened in music. We therefore will present only one sound for the letter a [ɑ].

1. Umlauts

Literally an umlaut is a mutated vowel. Its compound sounds are produced as follows.

a. ö or oe - closed, is transcribed [ø] and is pronounced with the tongue positioned for [e] and the lips positioned for [o].

Examples: Löhne   [lønə]
schöne   [ʃønə]

b. ö or oe -open, is transcribed [œ] and is pronounced with the tongue positioned for [ɛ] and the lips positioned for [ɔ].

Examples: Götter   [gœtər]
öffnen   [œfnən]

c. ü or ue -closed, is transcribed [y] and is pronounced with the tongue positioned for [i] and the lips positioned for [u].

Examples: lüge   [lygə]
             über   [ybər]

d. ü or ue -open, is transcribed [ʏ] and is pronounced with the tongue positioned for [ɪ] and the lips positioned for [ʊ].

Examples: hübsch   [hʏpʃ]
             Müller   [mʏlər]

e. It should be noted that ä is not an umlaut, but just one spelling of the sound [ɛ], or, when combined with u (äu), the sound [ɔø].

Examples: währen   [vɛrən]
             Träume   [trɔømə]

2. Closed Vowels

a. Most verbs maintain the closed sound of vowels in the verb stem throughout its conjugation, even when a double consonant occurs.

Examples: heben - hebt   [hebən - hept]
             loben - lobt   [lobən - lopt]

b. Vowels are usually closed when followed by h, which is silent.

Examples: sohn   [zon]
             kehle   [kelə]

c. Vowels are usually closed when doubled.

Examples: Heer   [her]
             Boot   [bot]

d. The letter combination ie, pronounced [i], is usually closed.

Examples: Tief   [tif]
             hier   [hir]

e. Vowels followed by a single consonant and a vowel are usually closed. (This does not apply to vowels in prefixes.)

Examples: Rose   [rozə]

                Leder   [ledər]

f. Final vowels in monosyllables are closed.

Examples: wo   [vo]

                du   [du]

g. u and ü are closed when followed by ch.

Examples: Buch   [bux]

                Flüche   [flyç]

3. Open Vowels

a. Vowels followed by two or more consonants are usually open.

Examples: Himmel   [hıməl]

                öffnen   [ɔfnən]

b. Vowels in most monosyllables ending in a consonant are open.

Examples: vom   [fɔm]

                mit   [mıt]

There are some important exceptions. When in doubt, consult a dictionary.

Examples: den   [den]

                dem   [dem]

c. The letter e in most unstressed prefixes is open.

Examples: entgègen   [ɛntgegən]

                erfàhren   [ɛrfɑrən]

4. The Schwa [ə]

a. The prefixes be and ge use [ə] for the pronunciation of e.

Examples: bedenke   [bədɛnkə]
gegeben   [gəgebən]

b. e in most final syllables el, en, and er is pronounced [ə].

Examples: Himmel   [hɪməl]
Haben   [habən]
vater   [fatər]

c. All unaccented final e's are pronounced [ə]

Examples: Stunde   [ʃtundə]
bitte   [bɪtə]

C. Consonants

1. **The voiced consonant sounds [b], [d] and [g] become unvoiced [p], [t], and [k] at the end of a word or syllable or in a final consonant cluster.**

Examples: hab   [hap]
kindbett   [kintbɛt]
legst   [lekst]

2. **ch has several pronunciations.**

a. When ch follows the back vowels a, o, and u, the sound is made by the back of the tongue and the hard palate (roof of the mouth) coming close together so that the breath passing through this narrowed area makes a sound of friction, [x].

Examples: Bach   [bax]
doch   [dɔx]

b. When following the frontal vowels i, e, ä, ö, ü , eu and äu, the fricative sound [ç] is made by bringing the

mid-point of the tongue close to the hard palate and
expelling the breath in a sound similar to the English
word <u>h</u>uman.

Examples: I<u>ch</u>   [ɪç]
                  Nä<u>ch</u>te   [nɛçtə]

c. The sound [ç] also occurs when i is followed by g at
the end of a word or syllable.
        Examples: ewi<u>g</u>   [evɪç]
                     Köni<u>g</u>   [kø…nɪç]

Please note that when a word contains ig followed by a
suffix containing [ç], the first ig will be pronounced
[ɪk].

Examples: ewi<u>gl</u>ich   [evɪklɪç]
                  Köni<u>gl</u>ich   [kønɪklɪç]

d. ch in words of non-German origin should be checked
in a dictionary.

**3. There are two possible sounds for the letter n
before g or k.**

a. They are usually sounded [ŋ].

Examples: si<u>n</u>gen   [ziŋən]
                sa<u>n</u>k   [zɑŋk]

b. In the ng combination the n is pronounced [n] and the g
is sounded when the syllables break between these letters.
Otherwise, the g is silent and the n will sound as [ŋ]

Examples: u<u>ng</u>efähr   [ungəfɛr]
                si<u>ng</u>en   [ziŋən]

4. r will be treated in two ways.

a. It should be flipped between vowels or at the end of a
word.

Examples: ih<u>r</u>e   [irə]
                vate<u>r</u>   [fɑtər]

b. It must be rolled when doubled and may be rolled for emphasis in other instances.

> Examples: He<u>rr</u>   [hɛr]
>   <u>R</u>auschen   [rɑoʃən]

5. The pronunciation of s can be determined as follows.

a. s is voiced [z] between vowels.

> Examples: Ro<u>s</u>e   [rozə]
>   ge<u>s</u>und   [gəzʊnt]

b. It is voiced when initial in a word or syllable and not followed by t, p or ch.

> Examples: <u>s</u>ingen   [ziŋən]
>   <u>S</u>eele   [zelə]

c. When preceded by a voiced consonant and followed by a vowel, s is voiced.

> Examples: Un<u>s</u>er   [ʊnzər]
>   Am<u>s</u>el   [ɑmzəl]

d. s preceding t, p or ch at the beginning of a word or syllable is pronounced [ʃ].

> Examples: <u>S</u>tunde   [ʃtʊndə]
>   <u>s</u>pringen   [ʃpriŋən]
>   <u>s</u>chön   [ʃøn]

e. In all other instances it is pronounced [s].

> Examples: sanfte<u>s</u>   [zɑnftəs]
>   li<u>s</u>peln   [lɪspɛln]

6. t has several pronunciations.

a. ti is found in some words borrowed from other languages and is pronounced [tsj].

> Examples: na<u>ti</u>on   [nɑtsjɔn]

patient   [pɑtsjɛnt]

b. th is pronounced [t] unless the syllables break between the letters.

Examples: Thal   [tɑl]
Goethe   [gøtə]
gottheit   [gɔt-hɑet]

c. tz is pronounced [ts]

Examples: sitzen   [zɪtsən]
trotz   [trɔts]

7. u after q is pronounced [v].

Examples: quick   [kvɪk]
Qualm   [kvɑlm]

8. v is pronounced [f]

Examples: vater   [fɑtər]
von   [fɔn]

9. w is pronounced [V].

Examples: Wasser   [vɑsər]
Wagner   [vɑgnər]

10. z is pronounced [tz].

Examples: Mozart   [motsɑrt]
Zier   [tsir]

11. Double Consonants
a. They are prolonged if they are liquid consonants
Examples: Himmel
Gesellen
b. Otherwise they are split so both letters are heard
Examples: mittel

Bett

IN STILLER NACHT
[ɪn ʃtɪlər naxt]
German Folk Song arranged by Johannes Brahms

In stiller Nacht, zur ersten Wacht, ein Stimm begunnt zu klagen,
[ɪn ʃtɪlər naxt tsur ɛrstən vaxt aen ʃtɪm bəgunt tsu klagən

der nächt'ge Wind hat süss und lind zu mir den Klang getragen;
dɛr nɛxtgə vɪnt hat zys unt lɪnt tsu mɪr den klaŋ gətragən

Von herbem Leid und Traurigkeit ist mir das Herz zerflossen
fɔn hɛrbɛm laet unt traoriçkaet ɪst mɪr das hɛrts tsɛrflɔsən

die Blümelein, mit Tränen rein hab ich sie all begossen.
di blyməlaen mɪt trɛnən raen hap ɪç zi al begɔsən

Der schöne Mond will untergahn, für Leid nicht mehr mag scheinen
dɛr ʃønə mɔnt vɪl untərgan fyr laet nɪçt mer mak ʃaenən

die Sternelan ihr Glitzen Stahn, mit mir sie wollen weinen.
di ʃtɛrnəlan ir glɪtsən ʃtan mɪt mɪr zi vɔlən waenən

Kein Vogelsang, noch Freudenklang man höret in den Lüften,
kaen fogəlzaŋ nɔx frɔødənklaŋ man hørət ɪn den lyftən

die wilden Tier traurn auch mit mir in Steinen und in Klüften.
di vɪldən tir traorn aox mɪt mɪr ɪn ʃtaenən unt ɪn klyftən]

FRENCH

The final language we are considering in this chapter is French. Here we will find some new challenges, but also new rewards. The most obvious language characteristic is the amazing flow of the language. Visually, French spelling is mystifying for the novice. Like other romance languages, syllables usually start with a consonant and end with a vowel <u>sound</u>. The word "sound" is important for orthographic spellings of words would seem to contradict this premise, but the actual sounds of the words (indicated by phonetic spelling) show that exceptions to this premise are rare. The legato flow of French is strongly influenced by this word structure. It is also strongly enhanced by the use of the following:

LIAISON—the sounding of a normally silent final consonant in a word that is followed by another word beginning with a vowel or mute "h".

When liaison is required, when it is forbidden and when it is optional will be discussed under rules of pronunciation.

Certainly another easily recognizable feature of the French language is nasality. When vowels are nasalized and when they are not is an issue deserving close attention and will be explained later in the chapter.

In general, French is a more forward language than English, with considerable lip activity and frontal resonance. Thomas Grubb illustrates this well in his text <u>Singing in French</u>, when he states,

"When a Frenchman is at a loss for words, which happens more often than one might expect, he rounds his lips in the position of a pout and drones on 'heu' for a moment, a sound that approximates the -er of English but which is much more frontal and without the final r. This rounded, definitely frontal utterance is the 'at ease' position of the French mouth and clearly illustrates the typical placement of French vocalic emission and resonance, which is somewhere between the upper front teeth and the base of the nose. In contrast, the English-speaking conversationalist fills his void with a heady 'um' or a throat 'ah'. His lips are flat and the resonance tends to remain somewhere beneath or in back of the nose." (Grubb, p.3)

As stated earlier, French is a language of challenges (as seen above) but also, it is a rewarding language for the singer. Once mastered, the legato line and the forward placement can lead to a fine vocal sound. The presence of many cognates (i.e. table-English, table-French) aids in its accessibility as does the fact that it is taught in many high schools.

Keeping a dictionary handy is absolutely necessary when using the following chart and pronunciation guidelines. Verb forms, final s in a word, mute and aspirate h are some of the items which will require dictionary help.

FRENCH PRONUNCIATION & I.P.A. SYMBOLS CHART

Orthographic French Letters	Phonetic Symbol	Orthographic English Spelling	Orthographic French Spelling	Phonetic French Transcription
Vowels				
a	ɑ	father	passe	[pɑsə]
a	a	between bag & bug	table	[tablə]
e	e	chaos	tournez	[turne]
é	e	chaos	blé	[ble]
ai	e	chaos	aiguisé	[egize]
è	ɛ	men	mère	[mɛrə]
ê	ɛ	men	même	[mɛmə]
e	ɛ	men	bec	[bɛk]
ai	ɛ	men	mais	[mɛ]
aî	ɛ	men	maîtriser	[mɛtrize]
aie	ɛ	men	paie	[pɛə]
aient (verb ending)	ɛ	men	saignaient	[sɛɲɛ]
ei	ɛ	men	peine	[pɛnə]
es (monosyllables)	ɛ	men	les	[lɛ]
e (final)	ə	petite	lune	[lynə]
e (final in monosylables)	ə	petite	que	[kə]
ent (3rd person plural verb endings)	ə	petite	parlent	[parlə]
i	i	police	il	[il]
y	i	police	lyrique	[lirikə]
o	ɔ	boss	robe	[rɔbə]
au (before "r")	ɔ	boss	Fauré	[fɔre]
o	o	rose	argot	[argo]
ô	o	rose	rôle	[rolə]
au	o	rose	l'autre	[lotrə]
eau	o	rose	beau	[bo]
ou	u	rude	tournez	[turne]
Mixed Vowels				
u	y	fühlbar (German)	vue	[vyə]
eu	ø	Höhle (German)	bleu	[blø]
eu	œ	bird	fleur	[flœr]

Semi
Vowels

i (before another vowel)	j	<u>y</u>es	b<u>ie</u>n	[bj<u>ɛ</u>]
il (preceded by a vowel)	j	<u>y</u>es	deu<u>il</u>	[dœ<u>j</u>]
ille (check dictionary)	j	<u>y</u>es	feu<u>ille</u>	[fœjə]
u (before another vowel)	ɥ	no english (y quickly moving to next vowel)	n<u>u</u>age	[nɥaʒə]
ou (before another vowel)	w	<u>w</u>e	<u>ou</u>i	[<u>w</u>i]
oi	wa	<u>wa</u>g	m<u>oi</u>	[m<u>wa</u>]

Nasal
Vowels

iñ	ɛ̃	**begin with [ɛ] and nasalize**	v<u>in</u>	[v<u>ɛ̃</u>]
im	ɛ̃	same as above	s<u>im</u>ple	[sɛ̃plə]
ain, aim	ɛ̃	same as above	p<u>ain</u>	[pɛ̃]
ein, eim	ɛ̃	same as above	R<u>eim</u>s	[rɛ̃s]
ien	ɛ̃	same as above	b<u>ien</u>	[bjɛ̃]
oin	ɛ̃	same as above	l<u>oin</u>	[lwɛ̃]
un	œ̃	**begin with [œ] and nasalize**	<u>un</u>	[œ̃]
um	œ̃	same as above	parf<u>um</u>	[parfœ̃]
on	õ	**begin with [g] and nasalize**	b<u>on</u>	[bõ]
om	õ	same as above	t<u>om</u>beau	[tõbo]
an	ã	**begin with [a] and nasalize**	s<u>an</u>s	[s<u>ã</u>]
am	ã	same as above	ch<u>am</u>p	[ʃã]
en	ã	same as above	t<u>en</u>dre	[tãdrə]
em	ã	same as above	t<u>em</u>ple	[tãplə]

Consonants

b	b	<u>b</u>ad	<u>b</u>leu	[<u>b</u>lø]
c (before a,o,u)	k	<u>c</u>ape	<u>c</u>ode	[<u>k</u>ɔdə]
c (before c)	k	<u>c</u>ape	ac<u>c</u>ent	[ak<u>s</u>ɑ̃]
c (final)	k	<u>c</u>ape	ro<u>c</u>	[rɔ<u>k</u>]
c (before i or e)	s	<u>s</u>ad	<u>c</u>ette	[<u>s</u>ɛtə]
ch	ʃ	<u>sh</u>ow	tou<u>ch</u>er	[tu<u>ʃ</u>e]
d	d	<u>d</u>o	<u>d</u>ame	[<u>d</u>amə]
f	f	<u>f</u>ire	<u>f</u>leur	[<u>f</u>lœr]
g	g	<u>g</u>rand	<u>g</u>rand	[<u>g</u>rɑ̃]
gu (before another vowel)			fi<u>gu</u>e	[fi<u>g</u>ə]
gu (before a consonant)			fi<u>gu</u>re	[fi<u>g</u>yrə]
gi, ge	ʒ	a<u>z</u>ure	lo<u>g</u>e	[lo<u>ʒ</u>ə]
h	—		<u>h</u>umaine	[ymɛ̃]
j	ʒ	a<u>z</u>ure	<u>j</u>ambe	[<u>ʒ</u>ɑ̃bə]
k	k	<u>c</u>ape	<u>k</u>ilomètre	[<u>k</u>ilɔmɛtrə]
l	l	<u>l</u>ime	<u>l</u>à	[<u>l</u>a]
m	m	<u>m</u>any	<u>m</u>ê<u>m</u>e	[<u>m</u>ɛ<u>m</u>ə]
n	n	<u>n</u>o<u>n</u>e	<u>n</u>o<u>n</u>	[<u>n</u>õ]
p	p	<u>p</u>et	lam<u>p</u>e	[lɑ̃<u>p</u>ə]
ph	f	<u>f</u>ile	<u>ph</u>ilosophe	[<u>f</u>ilozɔfə]
qu	k	<u>c</u>ape	<u>qu</u>el	[<u>k</u>ɛl]
q (final)	k	<u>c</u>ape	co<u>q</u>	[kɔ<u>k</u>]
r	r - flipped (classical)	t<u>r</u>ip	gue<u>rr</u>e	[gɛ<u>r</u>ə]
r	ʀ - uvular (popular singing only)		Pa<u>r</u>is	[paʀi]
s (between vowels)	z	ro<u>s</u>e	ro<u>s</u>e	[ro<u>z</u>ə]
s (all others)	s	<u>s</u>ee	<u>s</u>avon	[<u>s</u>avõ]
ç	s	<u>s</u>ee	gar<u>ç</u>on	[gar<u>s</u>õ]
ti (before most other vowels)	si	<u>s</u>ing	na<u>ti</u>on	[na<u>si</u>õ]
t	ti	<u>t</u>ea	<u>t</u>able	[<u>t</u>ablə]
v	v	<u>v</u>ain	<u>v</u>ol	[<u>v</u>ɔl]
w	v	<u>v</u>ain	<u>w</u>agon	[<u>v</u>ago~]
z	z	ro<u>s</u>e	<u>z</u>este	[<u>z</u>ɛstə]

General Guidelines to French Pronunciation

The following guidelines address only those spellings and sounds which require further explanation.

A. Stress and Accents

1. Syllables in French begin with a consonant and end with a vowel sound, contributing to the legato flow of the language. Also contributing to this smoothness is the fact that syllables are equally stressed except for the last syllable in a word which receives a light stress. In music, of course, elongation is not possible because the composer has written exact time durations for each syllable. In words ending with a schwa (ə), the stress will fall on the penultimate syllable, since the schwa is never stressed.

2. The following accent marks effect the vowels they mark as indicated.

  a. ´ - the acute accent usually indicates the closed sound of the vowel.

  Examples: vérité [verite]
              été [ete]

  b. ` - the grave accent indicates the open sound of the vowel.

  Examples: père [pɛrə]
              cède [sɛdə]

  c. ^ - the circumflex accent indicates the vowel o is closed, but the vowel e is open.

  Examples: tôt [tot]
              rôle [rolə]
              fenêtre [fɛnɛtrə]
              tempête [tɑpɛtə]

B. Vowels

1. The nasalization of vowels is accomplished by the lowering of the soft palate, thereby allowing the airstream to enter the nasal cavities. When this occurs

the vowel should sound nasal, but there should by no hint of an [n] or [m] following the vowel. Nasal vowels occur under the following conditions and are indicated when transcribed in the I.P.A. by a tilda (~) over the appropriate vowel (õ).

a. A vowel, followed by a single n or m or final in a word.

Examples: bon   [bõ]

parfum   [parfœ̃]

b. A vowel, followed by n or m which is followed by another consonant (except n or m).

Examples: chante   [ʃãtə]

impour   [ɛ̃pyr]

2. Mixed vowels relate directly to German umlauts and are produced the same way (see page 125). Only the spelling is different.

Examples: <u>German</u>   <u>French</u>

Höhle   [hø
lə]   bleu   [blø]
Götter   [gœttɔr]   fleur   [flœr]
fühlbar   [fylbɑr]   vue   [vyə]

3. The schwa [ə] is pronounced similarly to the German schwa with absolutely no stress. The lips are more rounded in French. It occurs in the following circumstances:

a. In spoken French most final e's are not pronounced. When sung, a final e becomes a schwa if a note is provided for it. In some cases, this will happen with a tied note. In the pronunciation chart and rules of pronunciation in this section final e is transcribed [ə].

<u>Spoken</u>   <u>Sung</u>

belle   [bɛl]   [bɛl]   [bɛlə]   [bɛlə]

Chapter 3 ... *Singing in Multiple Languages*

b. Before a consonant followed by a vowel

Examples: petit   [pəti]

              ceci   [səci]

c. Final in a monosyllable.

Examples: le   [lə]

              ce   [sə]

d. In words beginning with "ress".

Examples: ressort   [rəsɔr]

              ressac   [rəsak]

e. Final es in multi-syllable words.

Examples: belles   [bɛlə]

              chantes   [ʃɑtə]

f. In ent verb endings in the 3rd person plural.

Examples: parlent   [parlə]

              aiment   [ɛmə]

Since many ent words exist which do not fit the above condition, (i.e., many adverbs), a dictionary may need to be consulted.

Examples: différent   [diferā]

              extrêmement   [ɛkstrɛməmā]

4. Glides (semi-vowels)

a. Orthographic i, u, ou are vowels that sometimes function as glides. This happens when these vowels and vowel combinations precede another vowel. When this occurs, the first vowel is shortened and a glide results. That is: i becomes [j], u becomes [ɥ] and ou becomes [w].

Examples: bien   [bjɛ̃]

              nuit   [nɥi]

              oui   [wi]

The exception to this rule occurs whenever the second vowel would be a schwa. In those instances, the i, u, or ou remain as pure vowels.

Examples: vie   [viə]
              lue   [lyə]
              moue   [muə]

b. There are many times when il and ille combinations will be pronounced as the glide [j].

Examples: soleil   [sɔlɛj]
              fille   [fijə]

However, there are a few times when this is not true and the il, ille combinations retain the [il] pronunciations.

Examples: ville   [vilə]
              vil   [vil]
              tranquille [trãkilə]

To find which pronunciation is correct a dictionary should be consulted.

5. General Vowels

a. The sound [e] has several orthograpic spellings.

1. ai when final.

Examples: j'ai   [ʒe]
              gai   [ge]

2. e before a final silent consonant except s and t.

Examples: parler   [parle]
              chez   [ʃe]

3. e with an acute accent - é

Examples: blé   [ble]
              été   [ete]

Chapter 3 ... *Singing in Multiple Languages*

b. The sound [ɛ] can be spelled as follows.

1. e with a grave accent - è

    Examples: père   [pɛrə]
                         fidèle [fidɛlə]

2. e with a circumflex accent - ê

    Examples: rêve   [rɛvə]
                         tête   [tɛtə]

3. e before final pronounced consonants.

    Examples: éternel [etɛrnɛl]
                         avec   [avɛk]

4. e frequently before two or more consonants.

    Examples: belle   [bɛlə]
                         derrière [dɛrjɛrə]

5. aient in verb endings.

    Examples: auraient [ɔrɛ]
                         allaient [alɛ]

6. Most ai combinations within a word, including aî.

    Examples: clair   [klɛr]
                         maître   [mɛtrə]

7. es in monosyllables.

    Examples: les   [lɛ]
                         tes   [tɛ]

c. The sound [a] has the following spellings.

1. a with a grave accent - à and many other a's
Check a dictionary.

Examples: là   [la]
            parle   [parlə]

2. Many oi combinations.

Examples: moi   [mwa]
            doigt   [dwa]

3. An occasional e before double m or n.

Examples: femme   [famə]
            solennel [sɔlanɛl]

d. The sound [ɑ] has the following spellings:

1. Frequently a followed by s.

Examples: classe   [klɑsə]
            occasion [ɔkɑsjɔ̃]

2. Usually a with the circumflex accent (â).

Examples: château [ʃɑto]
            âge   [ɑʒə]

e. The sound [o] is spelled in the following ways.

1. o as the final sound in a word.

Examples: argot   [argo]
            galop   [galo]

2. o before the sound [z]

Examples: rose   [rozə]
            chose   [ʃozə]

3. o with the circumflex accent.

Examples: rôle   [rolə]
            tôt   [to]

4. au and eau.

Examples: sa<u>u</u>le [so̞lə]
      b<u>eau</u> [bo̞]

f. The sound [ɔ] is spelled in the following ways.

1. o in most positions not listed above.

Examples: b<u>o</u>nne [bɔ̞n]
      s<u>o</u>leil [sɔ̞lɛj]

2. au before r.

Examples: F<u>au</u>ré [fɔ̞rc]
      l<u>au</u>rier [lɔ̞rjc]

g. The sound [i] is spelled i or y.

Examples: <u>i</u>c<u>i</u> [isi]
      l<u>y</u>cée [lisɔ]

h. The sound [u] is spelled ou.

Examples: t<u>ou</u>rnez [tu̞rnc]
      g<u>oû</u>t [gu̞]

C. Consonants

1. Silent Consonants

a. In French, silent consonants mainly occur at the ends of words, and are generally confined to the consonant sounds <u>not</u> found in the word <u>careful</u>, i.e. [k] which can be spelled c or q, [r] [f] and [l].

Examples: la<u>c</u> [la<u>k</u>]
      co<u>q</u> [kɔ<u>k</u>]
      hive<u>r</u> [ivɛ<u>r</u>]
      che<u>f</u> [ʃɛ<u>f</u>]
      ba<u>l</u> [ba<u>l</u>]

b. The following exceptions should be noted.

1. When numbers are used in isolation, such as in counting, the final consonants are pronounced.

Examples: di<u>x</u>   [di<u>s</u>]

sep<u>t</u>   [sɛ<u>t</u>]

2. When numbers are modifying a noun, the final consonants are silent.

Examples: cin<u>q</u> jour   [sɛ̃ ʒur]

deu<u>x</u> bras   [dø bra]

3. The final **r** in words ending in **er** that are verb infinitives, will be silent.

Examples: all<u>er</u>   [ale]

parl<u>er</u>   [parle]

4. Nouns ending in **er** or **ier** which describe occupations usually have a silent final **r**.

Examples: boulang<u>er</u>   [bulɑ̃ʒe]

épici<u>er</u>   [episje]

5. Although usually silent, the pronunciation of final **s** is very capricious and a dictionary should be consulted when in doubt.

Examples: fil<u>s</u>   [fis]

san<u>s</u>   [sɑ̃]

6. Some final **z**'s are pronounced in proper names.

Examples: Berlio<u>z</u>   [bɛrljoz]

Met<u>z</u>   [mɛtz]

2. Liaison

a. When a normally silent final consonant is pronounced, this is described as liaison. It occurs when words are closely related (adjectives, nouns, etc.) and when the first word ends with a normally silent consonant and the second word begins with a vowel or a mute h.

Examples:	quand il	[kɑ̃t il]
	un infame	[œ̃n ɛ̃famə]

b. A dictionary will reveal whether an h is aspirate - which blocks liaison, or mute - which allows liaison. In either case, the h is silent .

Examples:	des hautbois	[dɛ obwa] (aspirate)
	les hommes	[lez ɔmə] (mute)

c. Certain consonants are altered in liaison. d becomes [t] ; f becomes [v]; g becomes [k]; and s and x become [z].

Examples:	quand il	[kɑ̃ til]
	neuf heures	[nœv œrə]
	sang impur	[sɑ̃k ɛ̃pyr]
	sans amour	[sɑ̃z amur]
	deux amis	[døz ami]

3. General Consonants

a. The sound [g] is indicated by the spellings ga, go and gu as well as g before any consonant.

Examples:	garde	[gardə]
	gothique	[gɔtikə]
	guide	[gidə] (note u following g is silent)
	grave	[gravə]

b. The sound [ʒ] is spelled in the following ways: gi, gy, ge and j.

Examples:	givre	[ʒivrə]
	gymnase	[ʒimnazə]
	gêne	[ʒɛnə]
	jour	[ʒur]

c. The sound [ɲ] is spelled gn.

    Examples: agneau   [aɲo]

                      digne   [diɲə]

d. The sound [k] has several different spellings.

    1. c before a, o or u and c final

        Examples: canne   [kanə]

                      cor   [kɔr]

                      culte   [kyltə]

                      roc   [rɔk]

    2. qu, (the u is silent) and q final.

        Examples: quel   [kɛl]

                      coq   [kɔk]

    3. k

        Examples: kilogramme   [kilɔgramə]

                      kangourou   [kɑguru]

4. All other consonants are pronounced as indicated on the preceding chart.

LA BICHE
[la biʃə]
Rainer Maria Rilke

O la biche; quel bel interieur d'anciennes
 [a la biʃə kɛl bɛl ɛ̃tɛrjœr dɑ̃sjɛnə

forêts dans tes yeux abonde;
 fɔrɛt dɑ̃ tɛz jøz abɔ̃de

Combien de confiance ronde mêlée à combien
 kɔ̃bjɛ də kɔ̃fjɑ̃sə rɔ̃də mɛleə a kɔ̃bjɛ̃

Combien de peur
 kɔ̃bjɛ̃ də poer

Tout cela, porté par la vive gracilité de tes bonds.
 tu səla prote par la vivə grasilite də tɛ bɔ̃

Mais jamais rien n'arrive,
 mɛ ʒɑmɛ rjɛ̃ narivə

rien n'arrive à cette impossessive ignorance de ton front
 rjɛ̃ narivə a sɛtə ɛ̃posɛsivə iɲɔrɑ̃sə də tɔ̃ frɔ̃]

SUMMARY

The purposes of this chapter have been to introduce the choral director to the International Phonetic Alphabet (I.P.A.); to begin the understanding of the IPA through the Italian language (the "singer's" language); and to present basic guidelines for pronunciation in Italian, Liturgical Latin, Spanish, Hebrew, German and French. In addition, several text samples have been illustrated; and a list of references for further study has been included.

REFERENCES—Chapter 3

ITALIAN

Adler, Kurt. THE ART OF ACCOMPANYING AND COACHING. University of Minnesota Press, Minneapolis, 1965.

CASSELL'S ITALIAN DICTIONARY, first MacMillan edition, 1977.

Coffin, Berton, Ralph Errolle, Pierre Delattre and Werner Singer. PHONETIC READINGS OF SONGS AND ARIAS. Pruett Press, Inc., Boulder, CO, 1964.

Colorini, Evelina. SINGERS' ITALIAN: A MANUAL OF DICTION AND PHONETICS. G. Schirmer, Inc., New York, 1970.

Errolle, Ralph. ITALIAN DICTION FOR SINGERS. Pruett Press, Inc., Boulder, Colorado, 1963.

May, William V. and Craig Tolin. PRONUNCIATION GUIDE FOR CHORAL LITERATURE, Music Educators National Conference, Reston, VA, 1987.

Moriarty, John. DICTION. E. C. Schirmer Music Company, Boston, 1975.

LATIN

Benedictines of the Solesmes Congregation (edit.) MASS AND VESPERS. Desclee & Co., Tournai, Belgium, 1957.

CASSELL'S NEW COMPACT LATIN DICTIONARY, first Laurel edition, 1973.

Hall, William D. (edit.) LATIN PRONUNCIATION ACCORDING TO ROMAN USAGE. National Music Publishers, Inc., Tustin, CA 1971.

May, William V. and Craig Tolin. PRONUNCIATION GUIDE FOR CHORAL LITERATURE.
Music Educators National Conference, Reston, VA, 1987.

Monks of Solesmes (edit). CHANTS OF THE CHURCH. Descleee & Co., Tournai, Belgium,
1953.

Moriarty, John. DICTION. E.C. Schirmer Music Company, Boston, 1975.

SPANISH

Adler, Kurt. THE ART OF ACCOMPANYING AND COACHING. University of Minnesota
Press, Minneapolis, 1965.

CASSELL'S SPANISH & ENGLISH DICTIONARY. 1986

May, William V. and Craig Tolin. PRONUNCIATION GUIDE FOR CHORAL LITERATURE.
Music Educators National Conference, Reston, VA, 1987.

Sobrer, Josep Miquel and Edmon Colomer. THE SINGER'S ANTHOLOGY OF 20TH CENTURY
SPANISH SONGS. Pelion Press, New York, 1987.

HEBREW

Baron, Joseph L. CONTEMPORARY HEBREW - 1: AN INTRODUCTORY COURSE IN THE
HEBREW LANGUAGE. Behrmen House Inc., New York, 1977.

"Hebrew Language", ENCYCLOPEDIA JUDAICA, Keter Publishing House Jerusalem Ltd.,
Israel, 1978. Vol. 16, pp. 1645-1648.

May, William V. and Craig Tolin. PRONUNCIATION GUIDE FOR CHORAL LITERATURE.
Music Educators National Conference, Reston, VA, 1987.

"Pronunciation of Hebrew", ENCYCLOPEDIA JUDAICA, Keter Publishing House Jerusalem
Ltd., Israel, 1978. Vol. 13, pp. 1120-1146.

"Transliteration Rules", ENCYCLOPEDIA JUDAICA, Keter Publishing House Jerusalem Ltd.,
Israel, 1978. Vol. 1, pp. 90-91.

THE UNION PRAYERBOOK OF JEWISH WORSHIP (Part II). Central Conference of American
Rabbis, New York, 1958.

GERMAN

Adler, Kurt. THE ART OF ACCOMPANYING AND COACHING. University of Minnesota,
Minneapolis, 1965.

Coffin, Berton, Ralph Errolle, Pierre Delattre and Werner Singer. PHONETIC READINGS OF
SONGS AND ARIAS. Pruett Press, Inc., Boulder, CO, 1964.

Cox, Dr. Richard G. THE SINGER'S MANUAL OF GERMAN AND FRENCH DICTION. G. Schirmer, Inc., New York, 1970.

LANGENSCHEIDT'S NEW COLLEGE GERMAN DICTIONARY. (Messinger, Heinz, German-English section, 1973; Messinger, Heinz and Werner Rudenberg, English-German section, 1978.) Richard Clay (The Chaucer Press) Ltd., Great Britain.

May, William V. and Craig Tolin. PRONUNCIATION GUIDE FOR CHORAL LITERATURE> Music Educators National Conference, Reston, VA, 1987.

Moriarty, John. DICTION. E.C. Schirmer Music Company, Boston, 1975.

FRENCH

Adler, Kurt. THE ART OF ACCOMPANYING AND COACHING. University of Minnesota Press, Minneapolis, 1965.

Bernac, Pierre. THE INTERPRETATION OF FRENCH SONG. Praeger Publishers, New York, 1971.

Cassell's New Compact French Dictionary, Fifth Laurel Edition, 1972

Coffin, Berton, Ralph Errolle, Pierre Delattre and Werner Singer. PHONETIC READINGS OF SONGS AND ARIAS. Pruett Press, Inc., Boulder, CO, 1964.

Cox, Dr. Richard G. THE SINGER'S MANUAL OF GERMAN AND FRENCH DICTION. G. Schirmer, Inc., New York, 1970.

Grubb, Thomas. SINGING IN FRENCH. Schirmer Books, New York, 1979.

May, William V. and Craig Tolin. PRONUNCIATION GUIDE FOR CHORAL LITERATURE. Music Educators National Conference, Reston, VA, 1987.

Moriarty, John. DICTION. E. C. Schirmer Music Company, Boston, 1975.

Rohinsky, Marie-Claire. THE SINGER'S DEBUSSY. Pelion Press, Inc., New York, 1987.

4. EAR TRAINING

The successful performance of choral music depends on perception. The more discriminating the perception of the listener, the more critical an audience may become. It is vital for prospective musicians to develop aural skills to the keenest level of perception so that performance, teaching and the composition of music will be at the highest possible standard.

In a real sense, a musician must reverse perceptions and learn to "hear with the eyes" and "see with the ears". The true musician must be able to pick up a score, look it over and "know how it goes" mentally. In addition, music must be heard in rehearsal or in performance and recognized, without a doubt, in terms of agreement with the printed score.

This chapter is designed to assist the chorister in the task of developing aural perception. Every chorister has a vast "memory" of aural experiences that have accumulated in the mind. They may be related to performances on a major instrument or voice; to symphonic and choral literature; or, to the milieu of cacophony that exists in the music of everyday life. As refined or as unrefined as these aural experiences may be, they are, nevertheless, part of the memory of the student. These aural memories need to be placed in some orderly perceptive network in order for the chorister to ultimately be able to claim music as a discipline. The accomplishment of choral music in performance is a concomitant experience made up of separate parts. This phenomenal experience, remarkable as it is, seems so simple to the fine performer; yet it is a simultaneous aural experience that contains, in addition to tone production, the accurate search for pitch, rhythmic and metric proportion, dynamic subtleties, timbre uniqueness and, if appropriate, harmonic balance. The inexperienced chorister may conclude that all of these factors are indeed present, however the seasoned listener may not agree.

Therefore, it is imperative for the chorister to experience ear-training as early as possible and attempt to master it as a musical discipline. The purpose of this chapter is to assist in that task; in other words, to try to bring order out of chaos in the area of ear-training. This chapter attempts to logically develop a solid foundation of ear-training within the tonal memory of the student so that it may be expanded throughout the period of training.

The demands of contemporary music cause us to turn to some consistent model that will be reliable. The traditional scale patterns came into usage centuries ago, but still give the chorister a fundamental "tonal frame" on which to build a foundation for ear-training. Mastery of traditional scales in all of the Greek modes, especially those we call "major" and "minor", is the first step in this development.

Each unit of this chapter is divided into specific objectives, assumptions and procedures. Exercises are presented in a step-by-step method, building a foundation with each sequential experience. A <u>Practice Guide</u> is listed at the end of each unit and a <u>Proficiency List</u> is also provided for the gradual evaluation and measurement of progress. The <u>Proficiency List</u> may be used as a self-quiz, a class test or in combinations deemed appropriate by the teacher.

This chapter may be used in its entirety as a supplement to voice class; in a fundamentals of music theory class; or within the choral rehearsal over a prolonged period of time. The text is essentially written for the student with guidelines and procedures for the teacher within the text and the appendix.

Additional materials for developing sight singing skills may be found at the end of the chapter.

UNIT 1
TONALITY IN MAJOR KEYS: MOVABLE "DO"

Objectives

To develop a sense of tonality in "the mind's ear" for music in major keys. To learn to utilize the movable do syllable system and numerical system in order to begin to develop a tonal frame-of-reference.

Assumptions

For the purposes of this unit, it will be assumed that the reader has no background in the formalization of a syllable/number system of tonality. If there has been prior experience on the part of the student, then it will be an advantage to review the logic of the systemized procedure that follows.

Procedure

A concept of tonality is based on a principle of a tonal system or tones that are related to each other in such a way as to be logical. History tells us that a tonality system was developed in medieval times by monks who needed some way to teach early hymn tunes and chant (Grout, p. 59) Their "hexachordal system" of six tones utilized the first syllables of their text in each of six phrases. This has eventually come down to us as do-re-mi-fa-so-la. Theorists have added ti for number seven, in order to complete the octave and resolve upward to do. This fundamental system now clearly identifies what we call the "major" scale and is the foundation upon which we can build a concept of tonality.

Exercise 1: Syllable Column

The Major scale is represented in an ascending and descending column, thus:

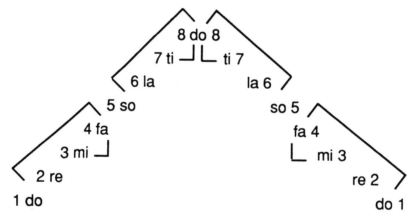

Sing several times from the pitch B flat (below middle-C), using syllables. Repeat the process using numbers. Note that half-steps occur between 3-4 (mi-fa) and 7-8 (ti-do). All other intervals are whole steps. The ancient logic of the Major scale produces two equal divisions, each with two whole steps and one half-step. These divisions are called tetrachords. In the major scale each tetrachord has the same step-wise proportion; no other scale is designed that way. Each is different.

Now, practice the scale ascending and descending from the vertical
column shown below. Skip from one degree to another in order to test
your ability to remember the tonal center — the sound of do.

PRACTICE COLUMN
(Major Scale)

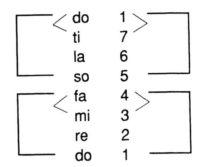

**Exercise 2: Major sequential pattern- - ascending and
descending.**

This exercise will assist the student in developing a fluency of syllables/
numbers that will, in turn, expand the tonal memory for a reliable
concept of Major tonality. Sing in a moderate tempo and in a light
voice, so that accuracy in pitch and interval will be at its best. The
sequence begins with one degree of the scale, adding each degree, one
at a time, thus:

Ascending sequence:

```
                                              so
                      ┌fa┐              ┌ fa  fa ┐
            mi        mi mi             mi        mi
    re        re  re      re    re        re           re
 do  do,  do      do,  do          do,  do            do,
```

etc., until reaching the upper octave do. Increase the tempo as rapidly
as possible for fluency development. Substitute numbers for syllables
in order to anticipate an important numerical relationship within the
scale system.

Descending sequence:

```
 do   do,  do    do,  do       do,  do              do,
  └ti┘  └ti  ti┘  └ti      ti┘ └ti              ti┘
            la       la  la        la        la
                 so               so  so
                                    fa
```

etc., until reaching the lower octave do. Increase the tempo as rapidly
as possible for fluency of development. Repeat, using numbers.

Exercise 3: Restful and restless tones

The tonal center of the Major scale is based upon do (tone #1). The first tone of a scale may also be called the tonic tone and it is upon this tone that one may build a tonic triad. Triads, as a group, will be explained later in this chapter. For now, please note that a tonic triad is a group of three tones made up of #1, #3, #5 of any scale. Therefore, in terms of syllables, the tonic triad in a Major scale may be sung do-mi-so. Practice singing this sound several times:

```
                    so
            mi              mi
        do                      do
```

Try it from different pitches in order to test your tonal memory. Does each one sound like a Major triad? Test yourself at the keyboard of a well-tuned piano. Use numbers 1-3-5 as well as syllables.

Each tone in the tonic triad in a Major scale may be called a RESTFUL tone. The triad is "at rest" aurally and seems to be final to the ear. All other tones in the Major scale, therefore, are RESTLESS tones that need to be resolved in order to satisfy the traditional expectations of the ear.

This concept of the need for resolution may be expressed within the syllable column, thus:

```
                        do
                          ↖ ti
                             la
RESTFUL TONES      {     so ↙        }   RESTLESS TONES
(tonic triad)                 ↙ fa        resolving toward a restful
                        mi              tone within the tonic triad.
                          ↖ re
                        do ↙
```

Sound the tonic triad on the piano and sing each RESTLESS tone, in turn, against the tonic triad, resolving appropriately as shown above. Do this several times in different Major keys, testing the development of your tonal memory for a concept of Major tonality.

PRACTICE GUIDE

1. Work with a partner; test each other.

2. Change starting pitch for variety and ease of vocal production.

3. Sing lightly. Volume is not as important as pitch and steady, moderate tempo.

4. Practice exercises #1, #2, and #3 thoroughly so that you have them in command before proceeding to Unit II.

PROFICIENCY LIST - UNIT 1   Date

1. Sing a Major scale ascending and descending   _____
      (using syllables and numbers).

2. Sing a sequential Major Scale ascending   _____
      (using syllables).

3. Sing a sequential Major scale descending   _____
      (using syllables).

4. Sing each RESTLESS tone against the sound   _____
      of the tonic triad and resolve correctly (using
      syllables, do this in three different Major keys).

5. Sing a Major tonic triad (do-mi-so-mi-do)   _____
      from three different pitches, chosen at random.

UNIT 2
THE MAJOR SCALES AND KEYS

Objectives

To develop the writing skill and the musical understanding of the Major scales in all keys. To relate this experience to the tonal memory of Unit 1.

Assumptions

It is assumed that some background in the notation of music has devloped; that the student may need clarification rather than instruction in fundamentals.

Procedure

The Major scale contains two equal tetrachords of four tones each. In the previous unit, the student has sung the pattern established by the Major scale in a variety of ways. Before the experience of melodic dictation, it is essential that the student has a precise understanding of all keys, Major and minor, and the scales thereof. This unit will cover Major scales; minor scales will be treated later.

Exercise 1: Notation for the Major scale - "C Major" - the perfect scale.

The C-Major scale evolves as the perfect example of two natural tetrachords that create the sound of the Major tonality. The following example, written in the treble staff using the G clef, and in the bass staff using the F clef, illustrates this pattern:

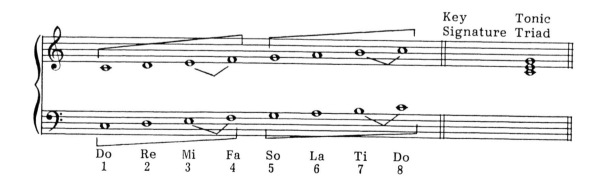

Each Major scale, regardless of key, has the same pattern of interval and tetrachord relationships. Steps 3 - 4 and 7 - 8 are always half-steps; all other degrees of the Major scale are whole steps. Transferred to the C Major scale, it shows that E - F (3 -4) and B - C (7 - 8) are half-steps and all other degrees are whole steps. The student should remember that E - F and B - C are the only <u>natural</u> half-steps found on the musical staff. Any other half-step must be created by altering a tone upward using a sharp [#] or downward using a flat [♭].

These altered tones provide the student with an opportunity to create a half-step between any whole step in order to write the proper scale in each key.

Write two examples of Major scales using the tetrachord model described above. The key "signature" is the result of any alterations written in creating the scale. Show the key signature and the tonic triad of each example:

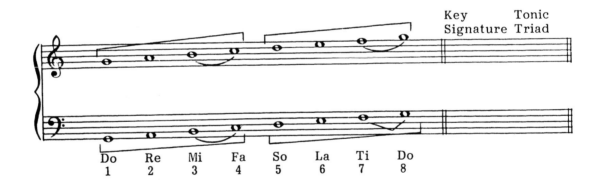

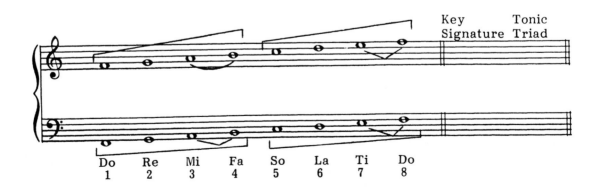

PRACTICE GUIDE

1. Remember, E - F and B - C are always natural half-steps; all other degrees of the scale are natural whole steps (in C Major).

2. In order to write a Major scale, the perfect tetrachord pattern of the C Major scale may be superimposed over any consecutive set of eight notes by altering appropriate notes to fit the pattern.

3. In the "mind's ear", sing the syllables do-re-mi, etc., as you write each scale. Allow the concept of the Major tonality to be reinforced in your tonal memory at every opportunity. It soon must be assumed.

4. Sharps (#) and flats (♭) are never mixed in Major scales. When utilizing sharps or flats they are always placed immediately <u>before</u> the note affected.

PROFICIENCY LIST - UNIT 2

Complete all Major scales using the tetrachord pattern shown in C Major. Use the accidental sharps (♯) or flats (♭) to complete the pattern (see appendix).

UNIT 3
<u>DEVELOPING TONAL MEMORY IN MAJOR KEYS</u>

Objectives

To expand the repertoire of exercises on vocal fluency in the use of syllables (numbers) and to expand the aural experience by singing in sequence the intervals found in the Major scale.

Assumptions

The student should be able to write and sing any Major scale with accuracy. Degrees of the Major scale should be known by number and by syllable; and, the key signature and tonic triad should be recognized and identified in any Major key.

Procedure

Sing from the column of syllables the following exercises and relate each one to the notation example shown in the key of C Major.

Exercise 1: Sequence in thirds

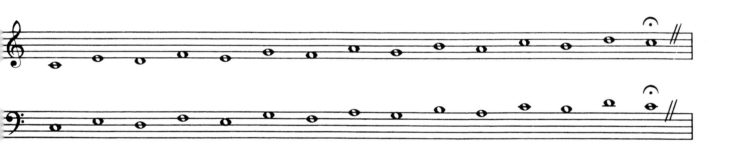

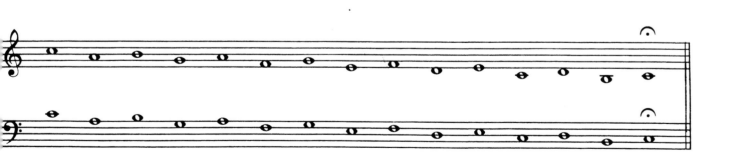

Exercise 2: Sequence in fourths

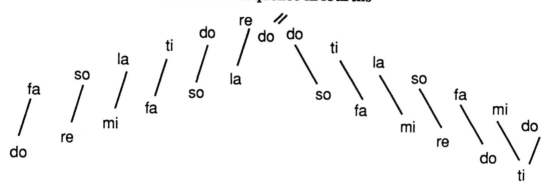

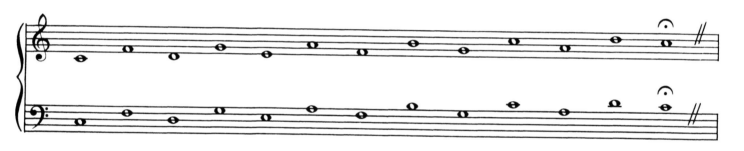

Exercise 3: Sequence in fifths

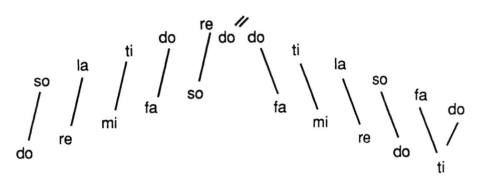

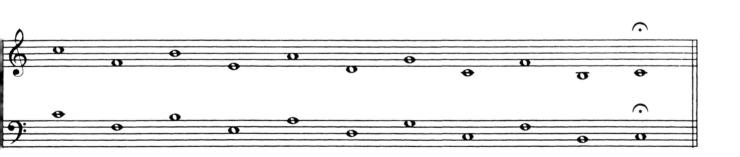

Exercise 4: Sequence in sixths

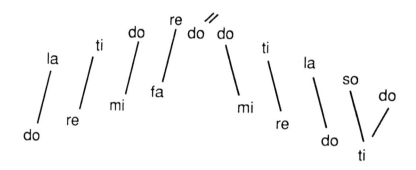

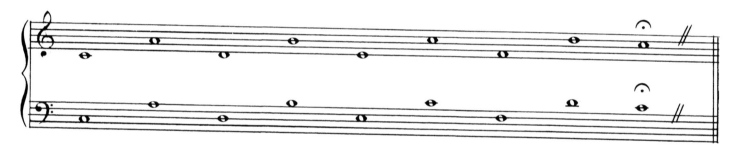

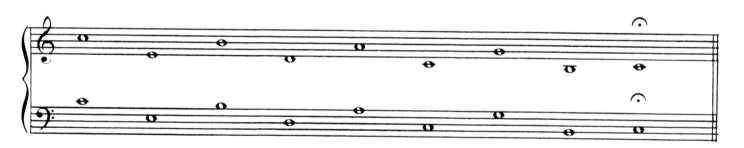

Exercise 5: Sequence in sevenths

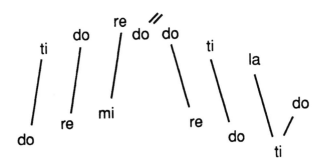

On each degree of the scale, a triad may be built. The tonic triad, as we have already seen, is built on the first degree of the scale and utilizes #1, #3, and #5, or every other note for a total of three. Triads may also be constructed in similar fashion above each degree of the scale; however, each triad does not have the same quality of sound. The qualities of triads will be discussed later in this chapter. If you have diligently practiced the preceeding Exercises 1-5 in this unit, you should be able to sing the following sequence of triads found in the Major scale. Remember to sing lightly, especially in the higher register of the voice.

Exercise 6: Sequence of triads - Major scale

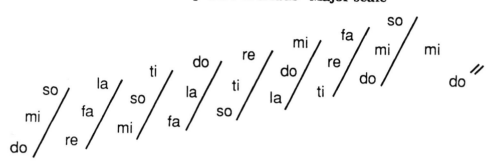

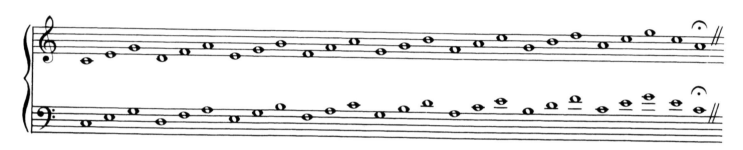

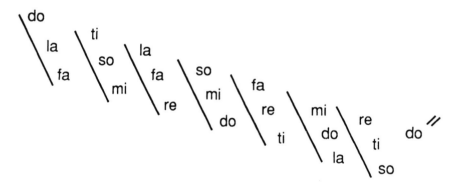

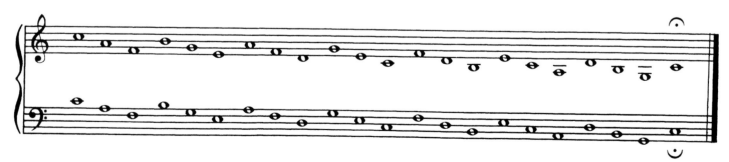

PRACTICE GUIDE

1. Memorize each sequential exercise using intervals (3rds, 4ths, 5ths, 6ths, 7ths). Check pitch carefully with piano or partner.

2. Practice sight-singing these sequential exercises from the musical staff illustrated with each one.

3. Practice the same sequential exercises in other keys.

4. Practice at an increased tempo; always be careful of pitch, diction and clarity.

5. Improvise exercises in syllables with a partner. For example, sing Exercise 6 as a variation while your partner sings only the scale. Sing Exercises 1 - 5 in contrary motion with a partner. What intervals are you creating by doing this?

6. As you sing Exercise 6, keep in mind that when a triad is built upon each scale tone, it is described as a triad in <u>root</u> position.

PROFICIENCY LIST - UNIT 3   DATE

1. Sing Major scale in thirds ascending   _____
     and descending.

2. Sing Major scale in fourths ascending   _____
     and descending.

3. Sing Major scale in fifths ascending   _____
     and descending.

4. Sing Major scale in sixths ascending   _____
     and descending.

5. Sing Major scale in sevenths ascending   _____
     and descending.

6. Sing sequence of triads in root position in   _____
     Major scale ascending and descending.

UNIT 4
DICTATION AND SIGHT-SINGING IN TONAL EXERCISES: MAJOR KEYS

Objectives

To take melodic dictation after hearing samples played three or four times. To further develop tonal memory in the Major keys. To be able to sight-sing simple music notation with accuracy.

Assumptions

It must be assumed that the student has a complete knowledge and understanding of all Major scales and key signatures; and, is proficient in the use of syllables (numbers) in interval and scale sequential exercises.

Procedure

Begin the dictation process by writing simple exercises in tonal relationships in Major keys. Utilize only whole notes for pitch location. Each thematic exercise may be written in one complete "measure". Rhythm and meter are not part of these early exercises. The most successful dictation usually follows a standard format. The following is suggested (you may want to develop your own):

"Given" information (by the teacher)

- number of measures (in the early exercises, one)

- clef sign

- meter signature (in the early exercises, none)

- key

- 1st note, supported by sound of tonic triad

- tempo, usually moderate

Preparation for Dictation

1. Teacher provides "given" information, described above.

2. Teacher plays through entire example; no writing.

3. Students <u>sing back</u> example on neutral syllable (la-la-la).

4. Teacher plays through second time, students writing. Students tap meter of exercise with forefinger on desk while listening. Students "sketch" location of pitches, using light manuscript.

5. Teacher plays example third time, students refine manuscript.

6. Teacher plays example fourth time, if necessary. No further opportunity to hear the example should be provided.

7. Students sing each example in syllables (numbers) as a class or individually.

Write as many exercises in tonal relationships as might be necessary to develop accuracy and confidence. Relate the sound of each example to the syllables and to the diatonic scale and/or the tonic triad. Samples have been written in each Major key and in the treble and bass staff.

PRACTICE GUIDE

1. Always take dictation in pencil, never with pen. The pencil allows for errors and accommodates the immediate need for erasures and corrections.

2. Review the <u>Preparation for Dictation</u> so that you might develop your own "system" for listening.

3. Practice with a partner from the same class. Compare simple examples and test each other.

4. Before writing, identify and notate the tonic triad on the staff with abbreviated notation, as a point of reference. For example:

C MAJOR

PROFICIENCY LIST - UNIT 4 (see appendix)

UNIT 5
METER AND NOTATION:
THE MEASUREMENT OF SOUND

Objectives

To experience basic notation and to understand the measurement of the musical line. To learn basic note values and to relate them to a meter signature. To learn basic rhythmic proportion.

Assumptions and Procedures

It is assumed that the student has an understanding of the treble staff, utilizing the G-clef; and the bass staff, utilizing the F-clef; and is familiar with the additional information that follows.

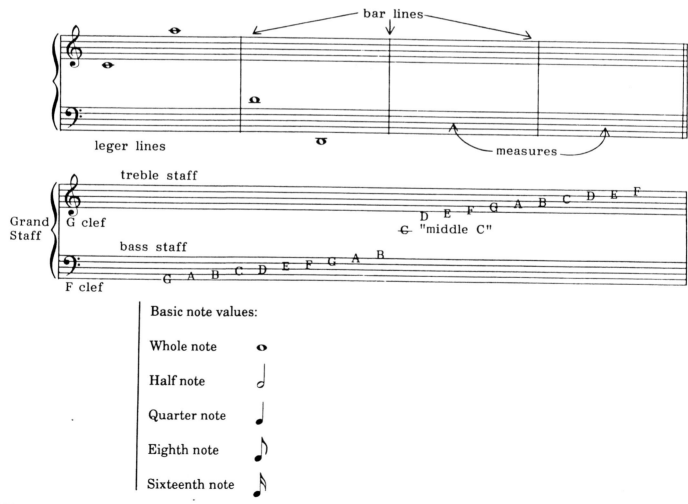

The relative value of these notes is determined by the meter signature, which may be illustrated as follows:

four beats in each measure (upper number) and the quarter note (♩) receives one of those beats (lower number). Therefore, with four beats in the measure there can be a maximum of four quarter notes.

This meter is often referred to as "common" time. Therefore, $\frac{4}{4}$ is sometimes written as C. When $\math₵$ (alla breve) occurs, it is simply $\frac{2}{2}$. Other combinations in 4 can be shown as follows:

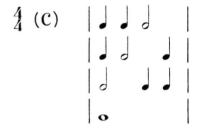

A numerical proportion may be shown by moving from the largest to the smallest value:

Samples of rhythmic pattern combinations with the quarter note as the "beat note" may be shown thus:

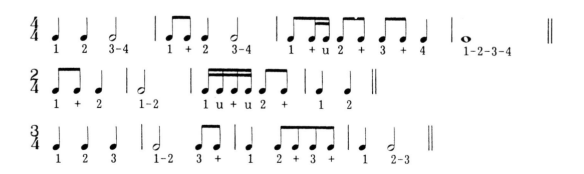

A very important factor in understanding basic proportion is the use of the dotted note. Whenever a dot is placed behind a note, it adds one-half the value of the note to its total duration.

For example:

Other examples of the dotted note:

Other meters are expressed by other meter <u>signatures</u>, for example:

$\frac{3}{4}$ = three beats in each measure and the quarter note receives one beat.

$\frac{2}{4}$ = two beats in each measure and the quarter note receives one beat.

$\frac{6}{4}$ = six beats in each measure and the quarter note receives one beat.

As the "beat note" is changed, the meter signature must also be changed. For example:

$\frac{4}{8}$ = Four beats in each measure and the <u>eighth</u> note receives one beat; and so on for 3/8 (three beats), 2/8 (two beats), 6/8 (six beats).

$\frac{4}{2}$ = Four beats in each measure and the <u>half</u> note receives one beat; and so on for 3/2 (three beats), 2/2 (¢) (two beats), 6/2 (six beats).

For the purposes of our exercises, we have limited our meters to those described above.

A concept of rhythmic proportion and the understanding of meter is based upon a basic mathematical relationship of sub-division. In the following examples; a rhythmic pattern is given for three meters: 3/4, 4/4, and 6/8, showing the conversion into related meters, in the correct proportion, but with a different "beat note".

1. Convert the example into related meters

Note that no rests are used in any example. The measures are fully sustained in note values. For the melodic dictation that follows there will also be no rests utilized, filling each measure with the melodic line. The beats of some measures have been sub-divided in order to use shorter note values.

PRACTICE GUIDE

1. Review basic definitions: treble staff, G-clef, bass staff, F-clef, Grand staff, middle "c", line and space names, measure, bar-line, leger line.

2. Review note values: whole, half, quarter, eighth, sixteenth, dotted notes.

3. Number each beat in exercise 1, 2, and 3, showing subdivision where it occurs.

4. Improvise several rhythmic patterns in 2/4, 3/4 , 4/4, 6/8 no longer than four measures, showing the numbered beats.

5. Complete Proficiency List - Unit 5 (see appendix).

6. Clap rhythms while "walking" the beat. Accent first beat of each measure.

7. Count the numbered sub-division aloud.

8. Combine walking, clapping, and counting in order to "internalize" the experience of rhythmic proportion.

UNIT 6
MELODIC DICTATION AND SIGHT-SINGING: MAJOR KEYS

Objectives

To take melodic dictation in Major keys, by listening to examples three or four times. To extend the tonal memory and the tonality concept; and include short thematic examples based upon the diatonic Major scale and the tonic triad. To be able to sight-sing these examples after writing them.

Assumptions

It is assumed that the student has had success with Unit 4 and has developed a reasonable tonal memory in the Major tonality. It is also assumed that the student has a basic understanding of musical rhythmic proportion, as described in Unit 5.

Procedure

The procedure for writing melodic dictation is similar to that described in Unit 4. Additional care should be taken for the rhythmic factor. The student should "keep the beat" with the forefinger at the desk, while listening to examples.

Several different keys are used in the following examples. Ten examples are in the treble staff and ten in the bass staff. A variety of meters is used and each melodic sample is diatonic in its design. Any intervals that occur are mostly within the tonic chord.

Follow the same procedure outlined in Unit 4 and carefully write examples 1 - 20. Teacher should accent first beat of each measure.

PRACTICE GUIDE

1. Review the Practice guide in Unit 4. These same procedures are appropriate here.

2. Clap (or tap) rhythms in review after each example is written. Listen for sustained tones (more than one beat) and the opposite (more than one note on one beat).

3. Continue to practice with a partner; both in writing and in sight-singing.

PROFICIENCY LIST - UNIT 6 (see appendix)

UNIT 7
DEVELOPING TONAL MEMORY IN MINOR KEYS

Objectives

To develop a sense of tonality in the minor keys. To learn the relationships between Major and minor keys. To expand the concept of tonality in order to master the three forms of minor scales. To be able to sing the three forms of minor scales with accuracy and consistency.

Assumptions

Success in the Major key exercises must be assumed. It also must be assumed that the student has control over the sequential syllable exercises described in previous units and has written all Major scales correctly as required in Unit 2.

Procedure

For every Major scale, there is a relative minor scale, indeed, <u>three</u> relative minor scales. Because of certain alterations, three separate scales may be written in each minor key.

The relationship of Major to minor is based upon the concept that if the minor scale is to be "relative" minor to a particular Major key, they both must share the same key signature. This relationship may be illustrated in two ways: the column of syllables and the scale structure.

Exercise 1

Review the column of syllables in the Major tonality. Sing the entire Major scale downward from do, continuing through the lower octave do to la.

Begin on la and sing the natural minor scale from la to la ascending and descending. Repeat this procedure several times until you have confidence in your performance. Check your accuracy at the keyboard in several different keys. Start in Major and convert to the relative minor by singing from la to la.

This exercise may be illustrated as follows:

The form of minor scale shown above is called "natural" minor. It contains no alterations and is constructed from la to la within the same key signature as its relative Major do to do.

Exercise 2

Review the natural minor scale by singing from the column of syllables from la to la. By making certain alterations in the natural minor scale, two other forms are possible. Before attempting those forms, it is important to remember that the natural half-steps in any column of syllables fall between mi-fa and ti-do. <u>All other degrees</u> of the scale are whole steps. Therefore, it is possible to sing half-steps between each of the others. Theoretically, these half-steps are called chromatics and will be treated in a later unit in this chapter. For our present purposes, only the necessary chromatics will be utilized in order to structure the other two forms of the minor scale: harmonic and melodic.

All three forms of minor may be illustrated thus:

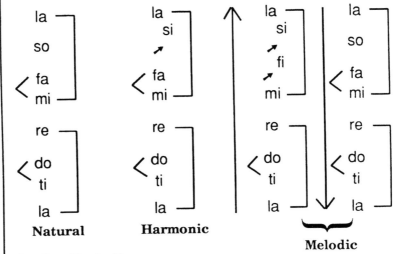

Another illustration:

Natural minor

Harmonic minor

Melodic minor

Harmonic minor is the same scale ascending and descending and has only one alteration: the raised seventh (1/2 step). This particular structure creates the sound most frequently experienced in minor tonality.

Melodic minor is one scale ascending and another descending. Ascending, the sixth and seventh are raised (1/2 step); descending, they are restored to their original state and, indeed, descend as the natural minor scale.

Each form will require practice and testing for accuracy and consistency.

PRACTICE GUIDE

1. Review Unit I and the concept of the use of syllables in the Major keys.

2. Combine the Major tonality (syllable column) with its relative minor. Improvise melodic exercises in both modes.

3. Please note that the lower tetrachord in each minor scale is the same; the upper tetrachord (harmonic) has the largest interval in the center; the upper tetrachord in the ascending melodic mi-fi-si-la sounds like so-la-ti-do in Major.

4. Improvise the entire sequence from a given pitch for "do", singing the Major scale ascending and descending; descending to the la, convert to relative minor and sing three forms of minor la to la ascending and descending, with appropriate alterations as needed. Practice with a partner and check for accuracy at the keyboard.

5. The tonic triad in minor is 1-3-5 of the scale as in Major; however, the tonality is different, since the tetrachord in the minor scale is structured differently. Practice singing 1-3-5-3-1 (la-do-mi-do-la) in order to master the sound of the minor tonic triad. Compare it with the sound of the Major tonic triad 1-3-5-3-1 (do-mi-so-mi-do).

PROFICIENCY LIST - UNIT 7   **DATE**

1. Sing the natural minor scale ascending
       and descending.   _____

2. Sing the harmonic minor scale ascending
       and descending.   _____

3. Sing the melodic minor scale ascending
       and descending.   _____

4. Sing a minor tonic triad (la-do-mi-
       do-la) from three different pitches.   _____

UNIT 8
WRITING THE MINOR SCALES

Objectives

To reinforce the concept of minor tonality by means of minor scale
notation. To relate the sound to the written music. To review the three
forms of minor. To write all minor scales in all keys with their relative
Major scale. To identify the tonic triad in Major and minor.

Assumptions

The student should know and be able to write all Major scales and key
signatures. In addition, an understanding of the relationship of Major
and minor keys through syllables should be clear.

Procedure

The minor scales contain two unequal tetrachords. One way to
construct minor scales is to utilize the tetrachord formula of the Major
scale. Another, and, a better way, is to relate the minor scales to the
relative Major, taking advantage of: (1) the shared key signature, and
(2) the few alterations described in Unit 7.

The relationship between a Major key and its relative minor (in three forms) may be illustrated thus:

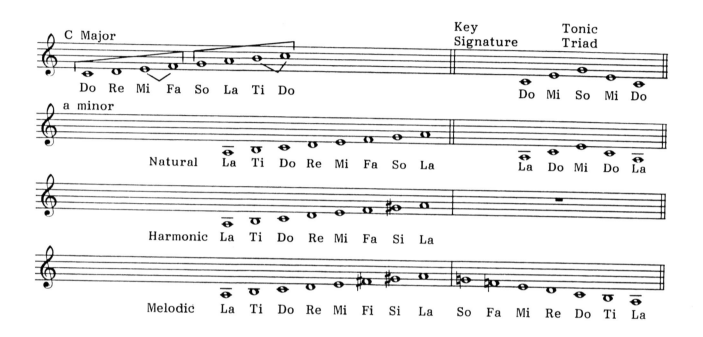

Observe the following in structuring the minor scales from a relative Major key:

- Since the Major scale runs from do to do, its relative minor will always be from la to la.

- The natural minor scale will always be from la to la without alterations within the same key signature as the relative Major.

- The harmonic minor scale will require only the raised seventh alteration (1/2 step).

- The melodic minor scale will require only the raised sixth and seventh (1/2 step ascending) and the restored (or lowered   1/2 step) sixth and seventh (descending). Remember, the descending melodic minor scale is, in fact, the natural minor scale.

- All three forms of minor generate the same tonic triad (la-do-mi-do-la or 1-3-5-3-1).

Since this illustration is in the key of C-Major and a-minor, no key signature appears. The following example is a more complicated one, and demonstrates: the use of accidentals (# or ♭) to structure the Major scale; the sharing of the key signature by the relative minor scales; and the alterations needed to structure the harmonic and melodic minor scales.

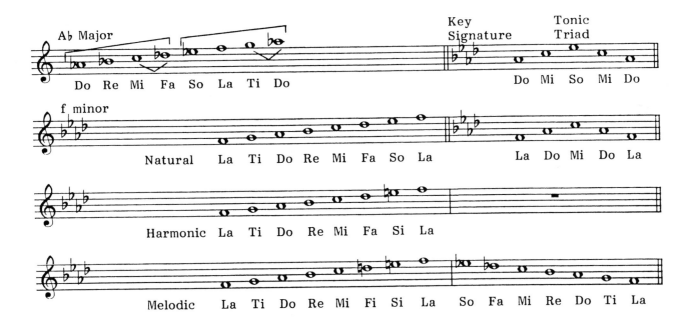

PRACTICE GUIDE

1. Refer to Unit 2 for a review of all Major scales.

2. Write all Major scales with accidentals, thereby deriving the key signature.

3. Illustrate the tetrachord pattern in writing Major scales.

4. In your "mind's ear" sing the syllables as you write each scale. This is particularly important in the three forms of minor, singing through the alterations.

5. Anticipate using double sharps (✕•) in some of the minor scales. A double sharp raises a tone two half-steps.

Complete all minor scales showing the relationship to the Major, sharing the same key signature. Use illustrations in unit 8 as models. Use proper accidentals in the Major scales. Use only key signature and alterations in the minor scales (see appendix).

UNIT 9
DICTATION IN TONAL EXERCISES, MELODIC DICTATION, AND SIGHT-SINGING: MINOR KEYS

Objectives

To take dictation in minor keys. To develop a tonal memory in the three forms of minor and to be able to distinguish each form "by ear". To be able to sight-sing examples after writing.

Assumptions

The student should have a clear understanding of the Major-minor relationship and an accurate ability to write all scales Major and minor. Also, the student should be proficient in singing the three forms of minor with consistency.

Procedure

The procedure to be followed for dictation in minor keys is similar to that of Major keys as described in unit 4 and unit 6. An additional thought process must take place in identifying the key signature prior to writing. Think through the relationship of minor to Major.

For example: If you are to take dictation in c-minor, in order to establish the key signature, call "c" la and sing up to do (the relative Major). do is clearly E♭-Major, which has the key signature of three flats. Therefore, c-minor shares the same key signature. You may need to do this several times before you actually "know" all key signatures in minor. The sooner one learns them all, the better.

The <u>tonal studies</u> that follow utilize no meter, only pitch location. Write whole notes indicating pitch, as you hear it. Each exercise is written in one complete "measure".

The <u>melodic examples </u>are written with ten in the treble staff and ten in the bass staff. Several keys are used as well as a variety of meters. They are designed to follow the diatonic scale or tonic triad pattern in order to help establish a solid tonal memory in minor keys.

PRACTICE GUIDE

1. The relationship from Major to minor keys, sharing the same key signature, is that la is always the relative minor to do (the Major). In numerical terms, the sixth degree of the Major scale is the relative minor.

2. Utilize the syllables as much as possible to re-enforce tonal memory in the minor tonality.

3. Develop a "number" concept in minor that clearly shows the vast difference in tonality between Major and minor. la becomes #1, thus enabling the student to sing the minor scales by number, ascending and descending, adjusting the pitch at appropriate places. Using numbers thus raises a consciousness of the raised seventh in harmonic minor, the raised sixth and seventh in melodic minor ascending, and the restored sixth and seventh in the melodic minor descending; as well as the lowered third in the tonic triad.

PROFICIENCY LIST - UNIT 9 (see appendix)

UNIT 10
CHROMATICISM

Objectives

To develop the ability to sing and write the chromatic scale. To relate the use of chromatics to sight singing and melodic dictation through the use of syllables in moveable do. To reinforce the use of chromatic alterations in the structure of the harmonic and melodic minor scales.

Assumptions

It must be assumed that the student has achieved all of the expectations of the previous units of study; and by involvement in singing, has "internalized" the characteristic sound of the Major scale and the three forms of minor scales by means of the Moveable do system of syllables.

Procedure

Review the syllable column of the Major scale, inserting the chromatic syllables. Note that the syllables read differently when ascending and descending:

```
                              do
                        li  ti ⌐⌐ ti   te
                  si  la                  la
              fi so                          le
            fa                             so  se
        ri  mi ⌐                              fa
    di  re                                     ⌐ mi  me
do                                               re  ra
                                                        do
```

Sing ascending and descending several times from a comfortable pitch in middle range, using a light voice. The priorities are intonation and accurate pitch, not volume. Reinforcement from a well-tuned keyboard is helpful as the singer reaches each note of the tonic triad do-mi-so in Major, la-do-mi in minor. Repetition and reinforcement are essential to reach the objective of successfully singing an accurate chromatic scale. After the aural concept of the sound of chromaticism has been experienced, transfer the sound to the printed score by singing the following. Whether the exercise is considered MAJOR or minor is irrelevant, since the chromatic interval of the half step will be the same throughout. What is essential in this aural and visual experience is the pre-determined expectation of MAJOR or minor as a beginning and ending; and the use of the syllables in relation to the printed page.

Begin the dictation of chromatic melodies using the Proficiency List - Unit 10 (see appendix). The melodies will be similar to those experienced in Units 6 and 9 except that there will be chromatically altered tones in each example. It should be recalled that in unit 9 the chromatic leading-tone was used in the melodic line of the minor keys. In other examples, chromatic alterations were used within the diatonic minor scales as described in unit 8.

Teacher uses the same orderly system of Preparation for Dictation as described in unit 4.

| Chromaticism in "MAJOR" Scales

1. C Major

Do Di Re Ri Mi Fa Fi So Si La Li Ti Do

Do Ti Te La Le So Se Fa Mi Me Re Ra Do

2. Bb Major

Do Di Re Ri Mi Fa Fi So Si La Li Ti Do

Do Ti Te La Le So Se Fa Mi Me Re Ra Do

3. D Major

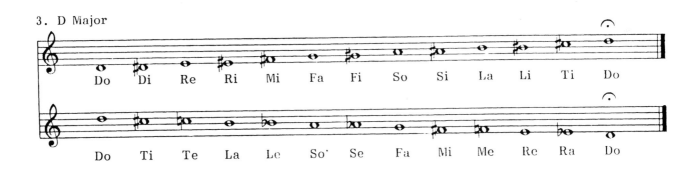

Do Di Re Ri Mi Fa Fi So Si La Li Ti Do

Do Ti Te La Le So' Se Fa Mi Me Re Ra Do

4. Ab Major

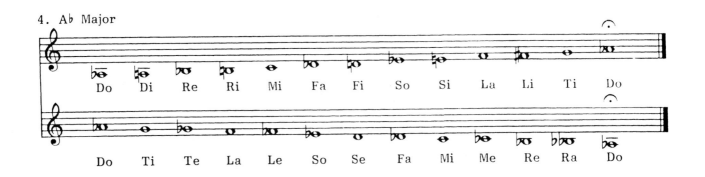

Do Di Re Ri Mi Fa Fi So Si La Li Ti Do

Do Ti Te La Le So Se Fa Mi Me Re Ra Do

CHORAL MUSICIANSHIP

| Chromaticism in "minor" scales

1. c minor

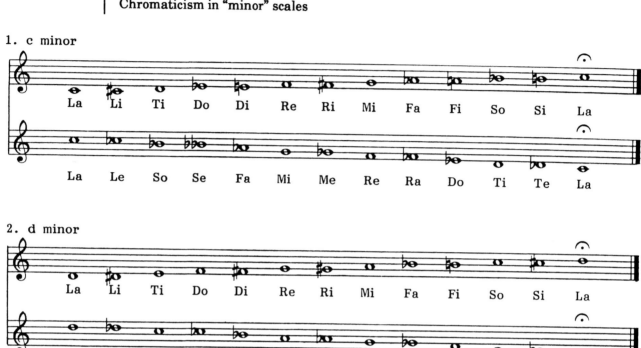

La Li Ti Do Di Re Ri Mi Fa Fi So Si La

La Le So Se Fa Mi Me Re Ra Do Ti Te La

2. d minor

La Li Ti Do Di Re Ri Mi Fa Fi So Si La

La Le So Se Fa Mi Me Re Ra Do Ti Te La

3. b♭ minor

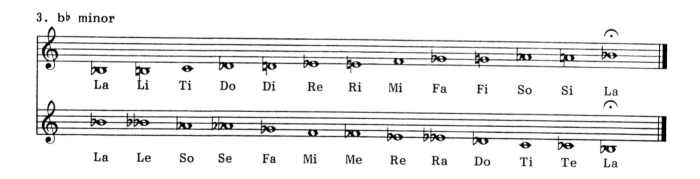

La Li Ti Do Di Re Ri Mi Fa Fi So Si La

La Le So Se Fa Mi Me Re Ra Do Ti Te La

4. b minor

La Li Ti Do Di Re Ri Mi Fa Fi So Si La

La Le So Se Fa Mi Me Re Ra Do Ti Te La

PRACTICE GUIDE

1. Review the chromatic scale, singing in syllables from do to do (Major) and from la to la (minor), ascending and descending.

2. Review the three forms of minor scales, singing in syllables, ascending and descending.

3. Practice with a partner, checking each other.

PROFICIENCY LIST - UNIT 10 (see appendix)

UNIT 11
INTERVALS AND TRIADS

Objectives

To learn to distinguish musical intervals by singing them on syllables within the context of the MAJOR scale. To be able to recognize them aurally and to be able to identify them ascending and descending. To identify aurally, and sing the triad qualities of MAJOR, minor, diminished and AUGMENTED, and sing the harmonic sequence of I - IV - I - V - V7 - I.

Assumptions

It is assumed that the student has experienced and completed all earlier units in this chapter. At this point, a review of units 1 and 3 is appropriate. What the student should have experienced in units 1 and 3 must now be the foundation of the next task: that of working with isolated intervals.

Procedure

All intervals found within the MAJOR scale may be sung and identified within the context of comparison with the TONIC TRIAD do-mi-so, thus creating an aural frame-of-reference for the student. As discussed in unit 1, the resolution of the restless tones against the restful tonic triad will aid the student in building a reliable tonal memory in which to work.

The intervals found within a major scale are classified as MAJOR (2nds, 3rds, 6ths, 7ths); minor (2nds, 3rds, 6ths, 7ths); PERFECT (primes, 4ths, 5ths, octaves). With certain inversions and alterations these intervals may become diminished or augmented. Our purpose here is to work with the basic MAJOR scale in the context of the "inner-ear", comparing each interval therewith.

Exercise 1: Singing the Intervals

The first experience in isolating intervals should be an aural one without manuscript—strictly "by ear". Sing the tonic triad do-mi-so in a comfortable key and identify the intervals by singing each one, as listed:

INTERVAL	ASCENDING	DESCENDING
Major second (M2)	do - re	re - do
Major third (M3)	do - mi	mi - do
Major sixth (M6)	do - la	la - do
Major seventh (M7)	do - ti	ti - do
minor second (m2)	mi - fa	do - ti
minor third (m3)	la - do	do - la
minor sixth (m6)	mi - do	do - mi
minor seventh (m7)	so - fa	fa - so
Perfect fourth (P4)	so - do	do - so
Perfect fifth (P5)	do - so	so - do

The prime and the octave need not be treated in this system. This experience is based upon the idea of comparison of the interval with the sense of tonality provided by the tonic triad of a given MAJOR key. Clearly, there are many ways to sing intervals. This suggestion is one means to systematically train the ear, so that ultimately it occurs without reference to syllable, number or letter name—the interval is "known". The next step should be associated with the written interval on the staff.

The following illustrations show the syllable designation for each interval and the written interval in a mid-range key for ease of singing. A variety of keys is valuable here so that the ear may move from one key to another. As each interval is sung, sound the TONIC TRIAD as a tonal reference, thus singing a "restless" tone against that "restful" triad; or, as in the case of some intervals, finding them within the tonic triad itself.

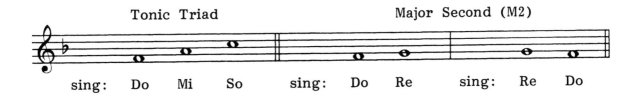

Tonic Triad / Major Second (M2)

sing: Do Mi So   sing: Do Re   sing: Re Do

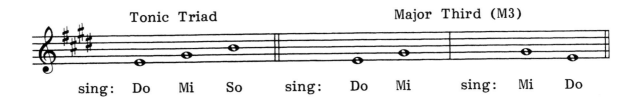

Tonic Triad / Major Third (M3)

sing: Do Mi So   sing: Do Mi   sing: Mi Do

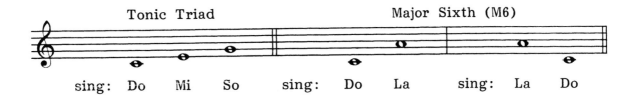

Tonic Triad / Major Sixth (M6)

sing: Do Mi So   sing: Do La   sing: La Do

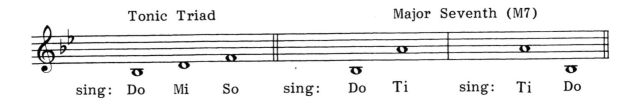

Tonic Triad / Major Seventh (M7)

sing: Do Mi So   sing: Do Ti   sing: Ti Do

Tonic Triad / Minor Second (m2)

sing: Do Mi So   sing: Mi Fa   sing: Do Ti

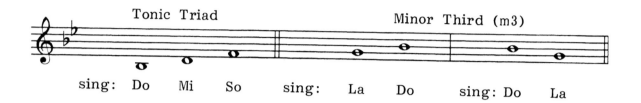

Tonic Triad — sing: Do Mi So — Minor Third (m3) — sing: La Do — sing: Do La

Tonic Triad — sing: Do Mi So — Minor Sixth (m6) — sing: Mi Do — sing: Do Mi

Tonic Triad — sing: Do Mi So — Minor Seventh (m7) — sing: So Fa — sing: Fa So

Tonic Triad — sing: Do Mi So — Perfect Fouth (P4) — sing: So Do — sing: Do So

Tonic Triad — sing: Do Mi So — Perfect Fifth (P5) — sing: Do So — sing: So Do

This sequence should be carefully practiced in several keys, so that the desired interval can be found in other ranges. Another technique that will further improve the skill would be to change the key between the ascending interval and the descending interval, thereby causing the singer to adjust within the "inner ear".

Exercise 2: Singing Triads

The four qualities of triads are: Major, minor, diminished and augmented. Each of these may be placed within the "inner ear" by means of relating their sound (hence the quality) to a sequence of syllables from within the scale system. This experience should be an aural one first before approaching the written manuscript. However, for the purpose of clarity, the syllables and the manuscript are presented together, as follows:

MAJOR Triads

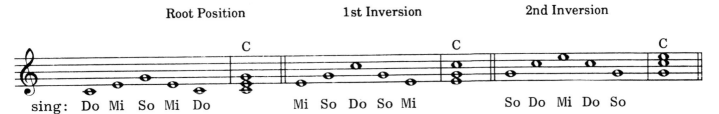

Sing the MAJOR triad sequence again, keeping the same pitch as the lower tone, thereby changing keys within each inversion, thus causing the "inner-ear" to make the adjustment in tonality.

Thus the lower tone becomes a common pitch for each triad, causing the "inner ear" to think in three keys in MAJOR tonality.

Minor Triads

Root Position   1st Inversion   2nd Inversion

sing: La Do Mi Do La   Do Mi La Mi Do   Mi La Do La Mi

Following the same procedure as in the MAJOR triads, sing the minor triads in the same key with two inversions, as shown above. Then sing the minor triads with the same lower tone as the common tone, thus singing in three minor keys.

sing: La Do Mi Do La   Do Mi La Mi Do   Mi La Do La Mi

Diminished Triads

The sound of the diminished triad is found on the seventh degree of the MAJOR scale and is heard by singing the syllables ti-re-fa as shown below. Note that the intervals are two equal minor thirds.

sing: Ti   Re   Fa   Re   Ti   Ti   Re   Fa   Re   Ti

These are only two illustrations of the sound of the diminished triad. Sing the sequence ti-re-fa-re-ti from any comfortable pitch in order to experience a variety of keys and to increase the ability of the "inner ear" to function.

Augmented Triads

The sound of the AUGMENTED triad is found by utilizing a chromatic alteration of a MAJOR triad. The Augmented triad, like the diminished triad, is made up of two equal intervals; in this case, two MAJOR thirds, thus the chromatic alteration. Sing the syllables do-mi-si, as shown below:

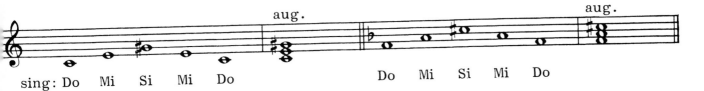

sing: Do Mi Si Mi Do   Do Mi Si Mi Do

As in the case of the diminished triad, it is a good idea to change the pitch of the starting tone and sing the AUGMENTED triad from several pitches, thus challenging the "inner ear".

In each case, both diminished and AUGMENTED, singing them in isolation is one thing, but relating them to a tonality is another. This can be achieved by <u>resolving</u> them from any pitch to the appropriate key. For example, the diminished ti-re-fa-re-ti can immediately resolve to do-mi-so-mi-do in the MAJOR key. In singing the augmented triad, we will always find an augmented triad as the third degree of the harmonic minor scale, thereby, making it possible to resolve, in minor, from do-mi-si to la-mi-do-la in a descending pattern, thereby relating the AUGMENTED triad to a minor tonality.

Each of these resolutions is illustrated below. Again, try it from several comfortable pitches in order to challenge the "inner ear".

Diminished Triad with Major Triad Resolution

sing: Ti Re Fa Re Ti   Do Mi So Mi Do   Ti Re Fa Re Ti   Do Mi So Mi Do

Augmented Triad with Minor Triad Resolution

sing: Do Mi Si   La Mi Do La   Do Mi Si   La Mi Do La

Singing the Harmonic Sequence: I-IV-I-V-V7-I

One of the advantages of familiarization with MOVEABLE do syllables
is the tonal memory that can be developed in the "inner ear", thus
making it possible for a singer to always be able to relate to a particular
key. Hundreds of folk songs are based upon the use of the primary
triads to create the harmonic structure (tonic - I, sub-dominant - IV,
dominant - V). The singer's ear can be developed so that the entire
sequence of I-IV-I-V-V7-I can be sung in arpeggio as an aural challenge.
A sample is shown below, both in MAJOR and in minor. The singing of
the syllables alone should precede the reading of the manuscript, so
that the experience can take place before the theory is applied. In other
words, the ear before the eye.

<u>MAJOR</u>

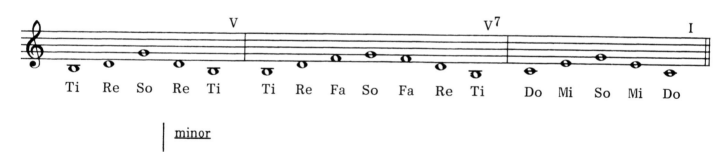

<u>minor</u>

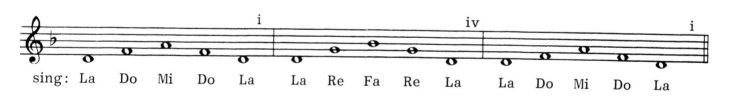

SUMMARY

The purpose of this chapter has been to bring together, in an orderly fashion, certain aural and written experiences that will assist the singer in the development of the "inner ear"; and to cause the singer to be more acutely aware of tonality in the major and minor modes. Any development, of necessity, is a gradual progression of experiences, each dependent on the other, but the emphasis should always be on the aural experience first and the visual, written experience later. In the final analysis, the use of syllables, numbers or letter names is only an aid to learning. A large number of concomitant experiences make up the concept-of-the-whole involved in ear-training: rhythmic proportion, melodic line, interval recognition, pitch and intonation, major and minor tonalities, triad qualities and basic harmonic progressions—all contributing to the ability to "see with the ears and hear with the eyes".

REFERENCES—Chapter 4

Berkowitz, Sol, Gabriel Fontrier and Leo Kraft. A NEW APPROACH TO SIGHT SINGING. W. W. Norton., New York

Boyd, Jack. TEACHING CHORAL SIGHT-READING. Mark Foster Music Company. Champaign, Illinois., 1981.

Cooper, Irvin and Karl O. Kuersteiner. TEACHING JUNIOR HIGH SCHOOL MUSIC. Allyn and Bacon, Boston., 1965.

Garretson, Robert L. CONDUCTING CHORAL MUSIC. Allyn and Bacon, Inc., Boston, 1975.

Grout, Donald J. A History of Western Music. W. W. Norton., N.Y., 1973. pp. 59-61.

Heffernan, Charles W. CHORAL MUSIC: TECHNIQUE AND ARTISTRY. Prentice-Hall, Inc., Englewood Cliffs, NJ, 1982.

Kodaly, Zoltan. LET US SING CORRECTLY. Boosey & Hawkes. Farmingdale, NY, 1961.

Phillips, Kenneth H. "Sight-Singing: Where Have We Been? Where Are We Going?" THE CHORAL JOURNAL. Vol. XXIV, No. 6, February, 1984, Pp 11-17.

Roe, Paul F. CHORAL MUSIC EDUCATION. Prentice-Hall, Inc., Englewood Cliffs, NJ, 1970.

Swanson, Frederick J. MUSIC TEACHING IN THE JUNIOR HIGH AND MIDDLE SCHOOL. Prentice Hall, Inc., Englewood Cliffs, NJ, 1973, Chapter 11.

Trubitt, Allen and Robert S. Hines. EAR TRAINING AND SIGHT-SINGING. Schirmer Books, NY, 1979.

APPENDIX

CHAPTER 4: EAR TRAINING (STUDENT WORKSHEETS)

Unit 2 - Proficiency List: Major Scales & Keys

Unit 4 - Tonal Studies in Major

Unit 5 - Proficiency List: Rhythmic Proportion & Meter
Rhythmic Patterns

Unit 6 - Proficiency List: Diatonic Melodies - Major (Treble)
Diatonic Melodies - Major (Bass)

Unit 8 - Proficiency List: minor scales & keys

Unit 9 - Proficiency List A: Tonal Studies in minor
Proficiency List B: Diatonic Melodies: minor (Treble)
Proficiency List C: Diatonic Melodies: minor(Bass)

Unit 10 - Proficiency List: Diatonic Melodies Using Chromaticism
Chromaticism in Major Scales
Chromaticism in minor Scales

Unit 2 - Proficiency List: Major Scales & Keys

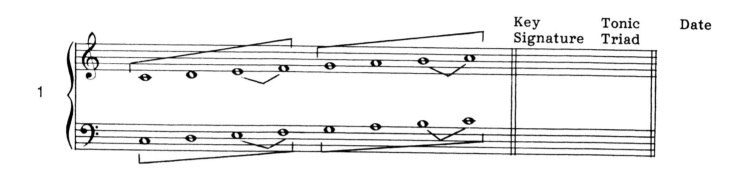

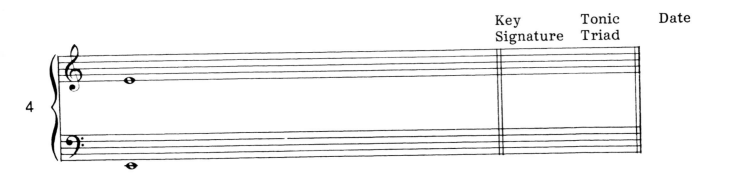

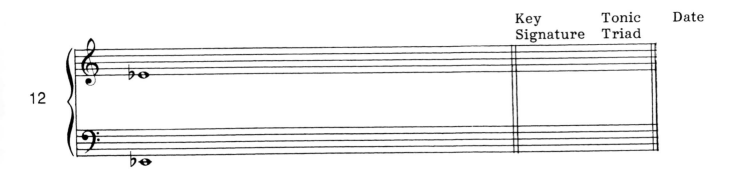

Unit 4 - Proficiency List: Tonal Studies in Major

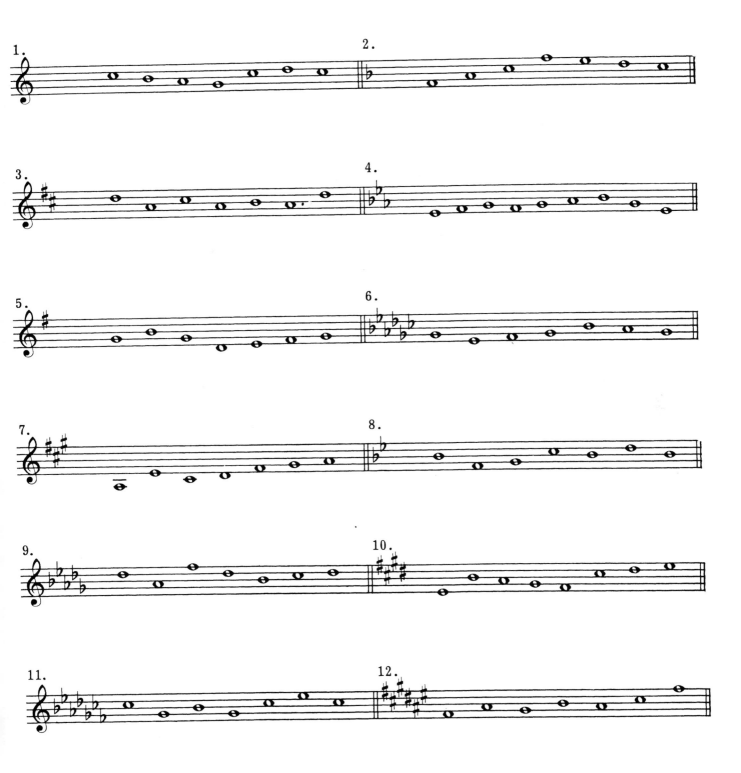

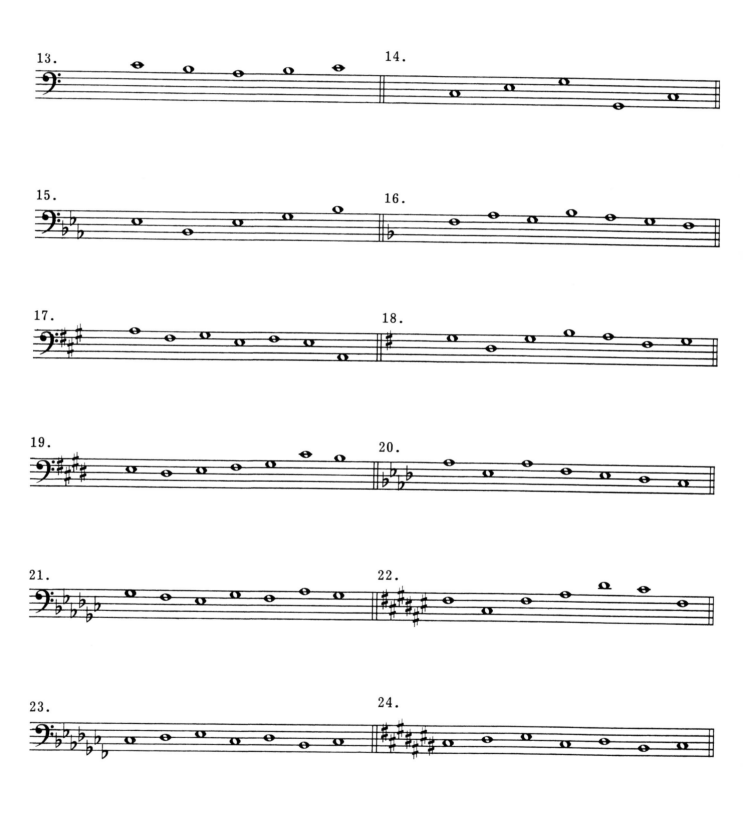

Unit 5 - Proficiency List: Rhythmic Proportion & Meter
Rhythmic Patterns

1. Rhythmic proportion and meter

2.

3.

4.

5.

6.

Rhythmic Patterns

1. Convert the example into related meters

Unit 6 - Proficiency List: Diatonic Melodies - Major (Treble)

Diatonic Melodies - Major (Bass)

1.

2.

3.

4.

5.

6.

7.

8.

9.

10.

Unit 8 - Proficiency List: minor scales & keys

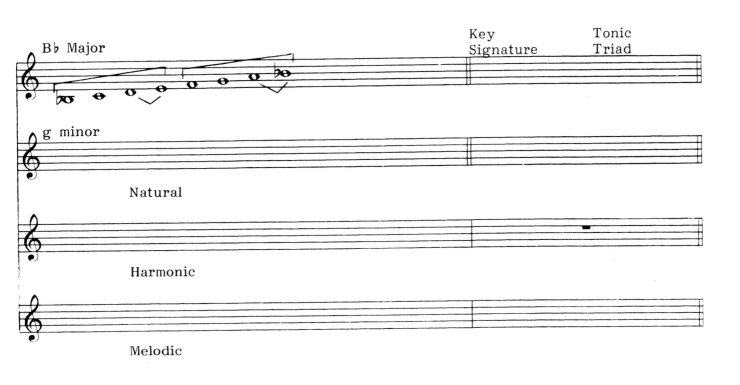

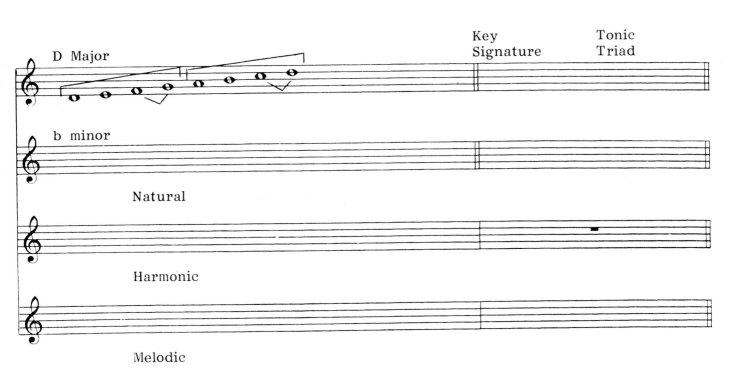

CHORAL MUSICIANSHIP

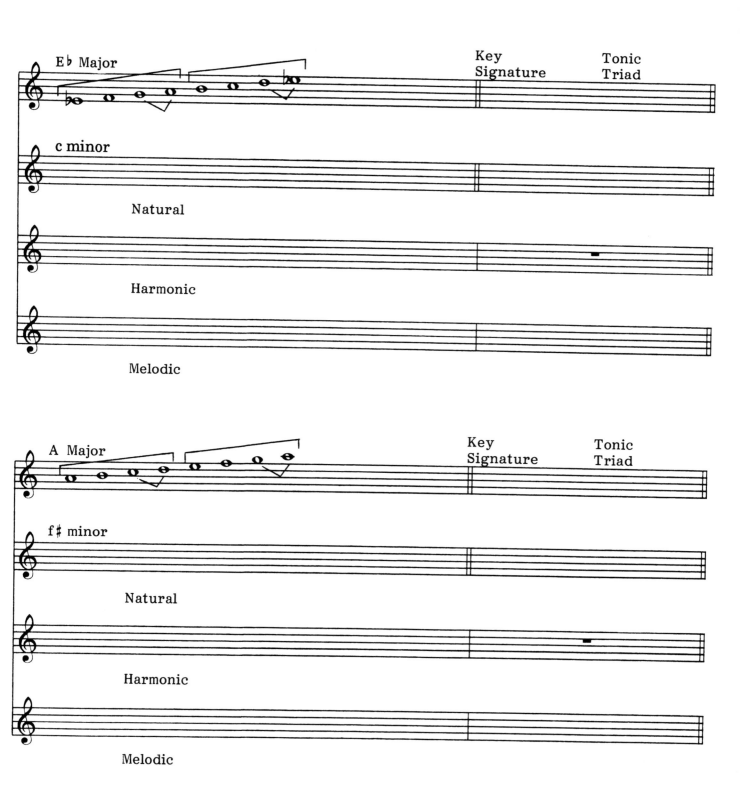

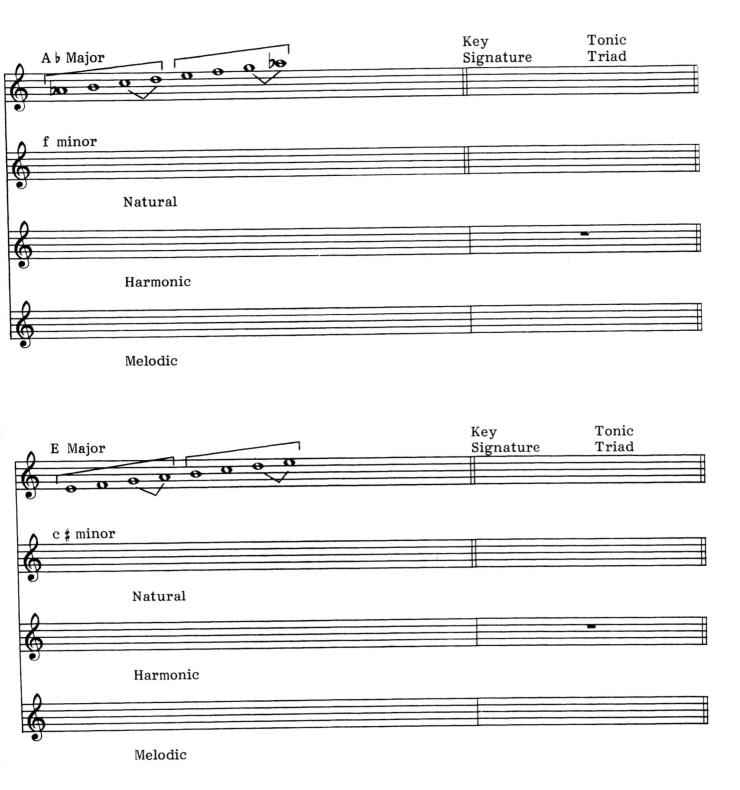

A♭ Major   Key Signature   Tonic Triad

f minor

Natural

Harmonic

Melodic

E Major   Key Signature   Tonic Triad

c♯ minor

Natural

Harmonic

Melodic

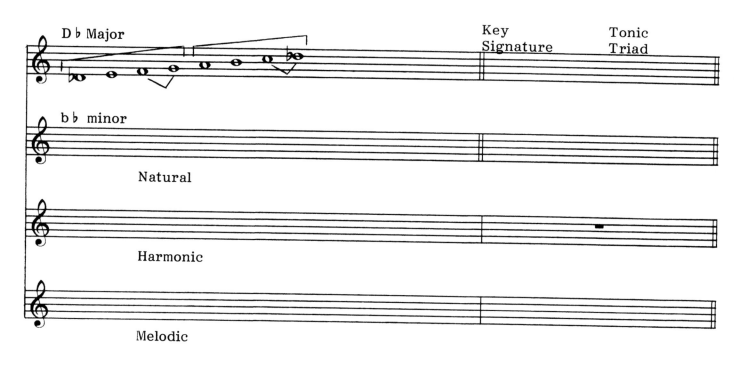

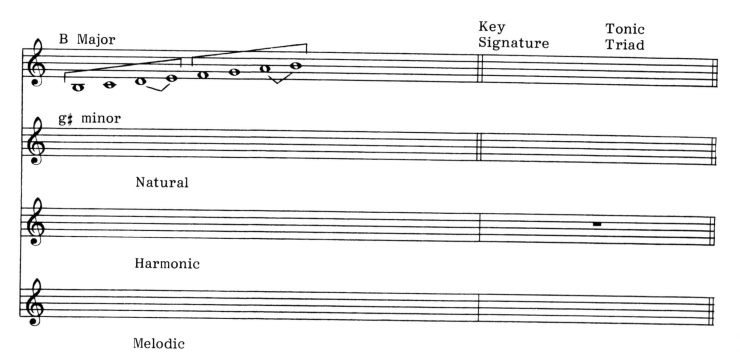

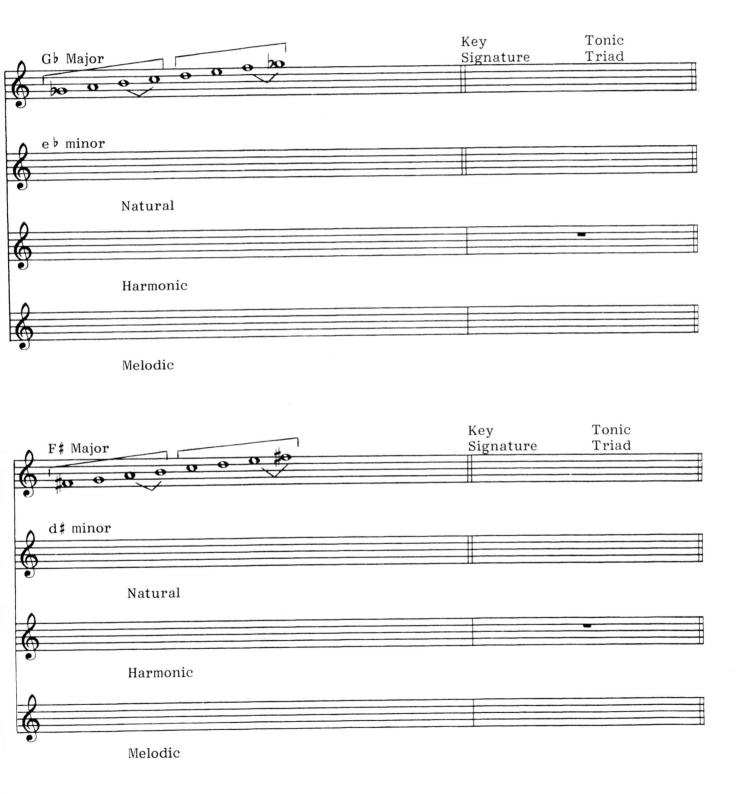

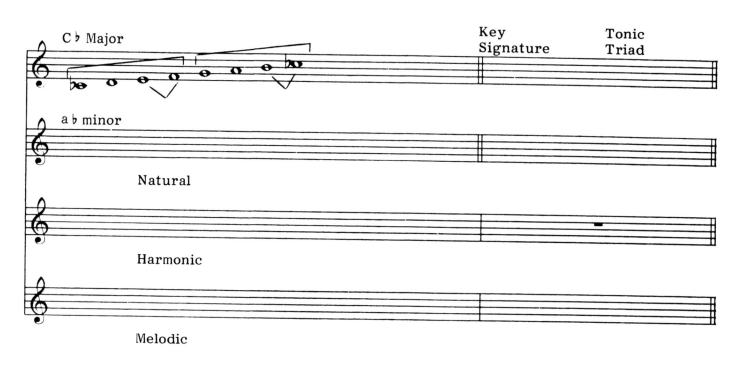

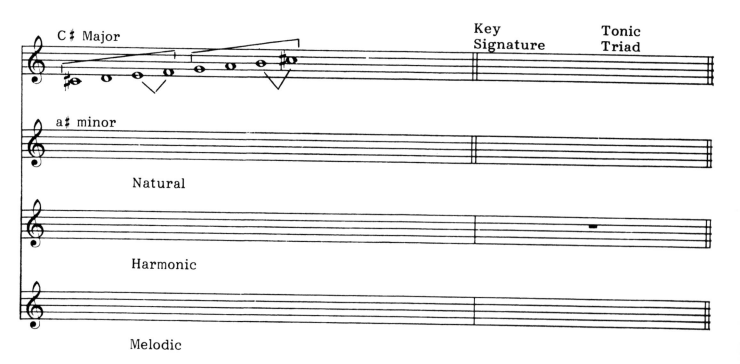

Unit 9 - Proficiency List A: Tonal Studies in minor

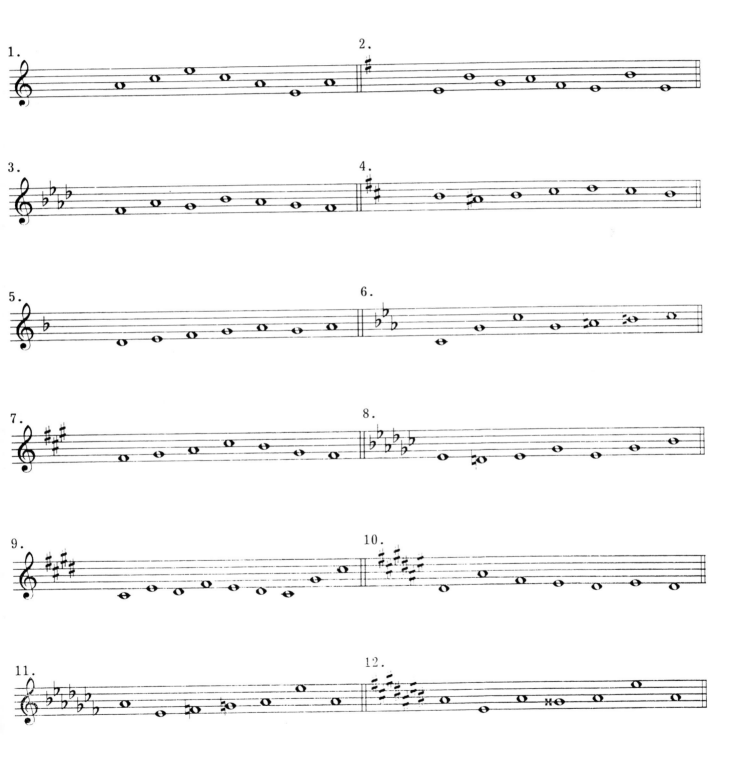

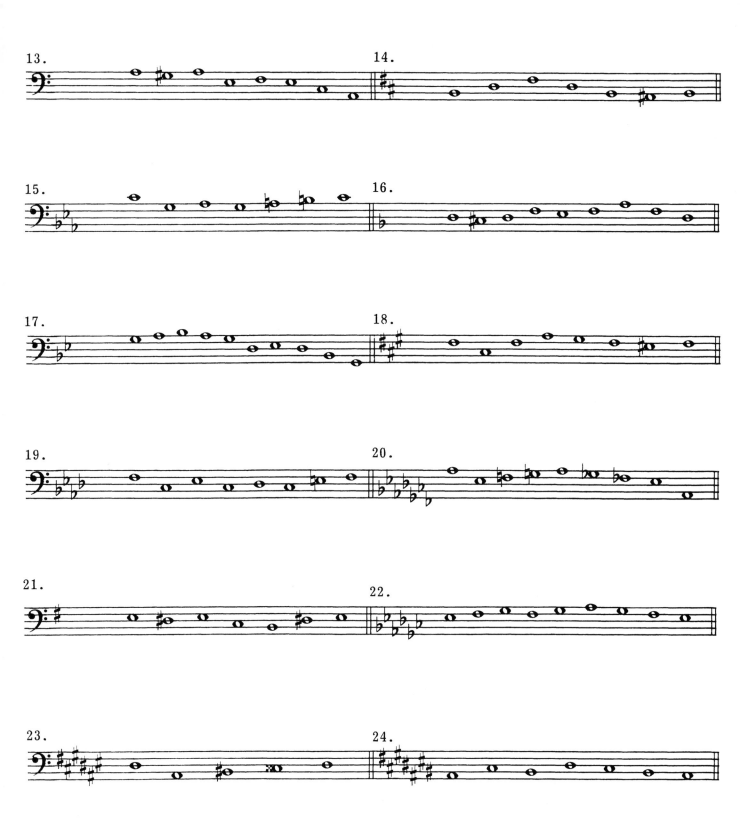

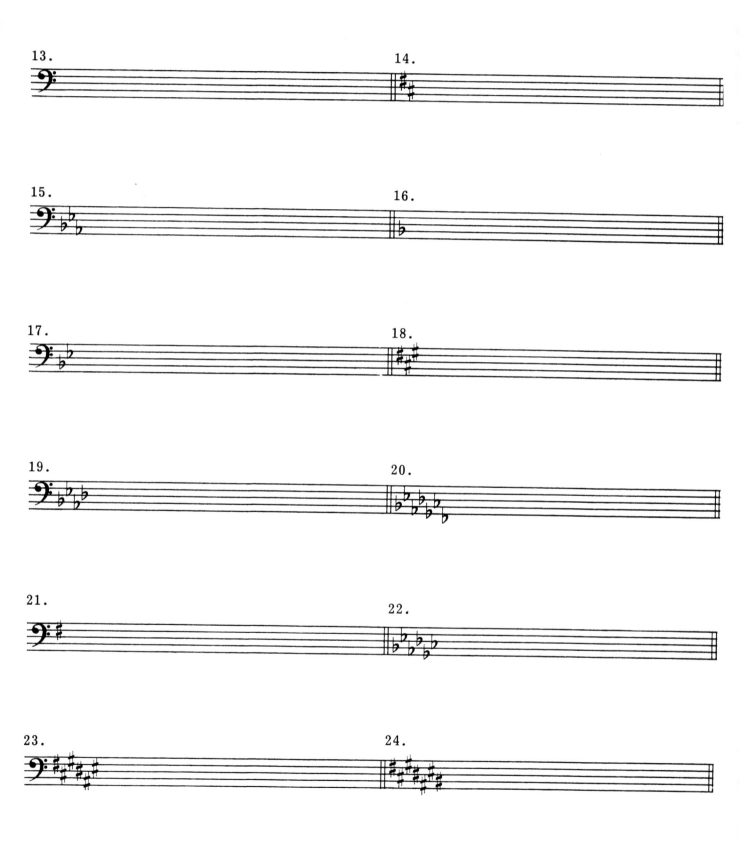

Unit 9 - Proficiency List B: Diatonic Melodies: minor (Treble)

CHORAL MUSICIANSHIP

Unit 9 - Proficiency List C: Diatonic Melodies: minor (Bass)

CHORAL MUSICIANSHIP

1.

2.

3.

4.

5.

6.

7.

8.

9.

10.

Unit 10 - Proficiency List: Diatonic Melodies Using Chromaticism

CHORAL MUSICIANSHIP

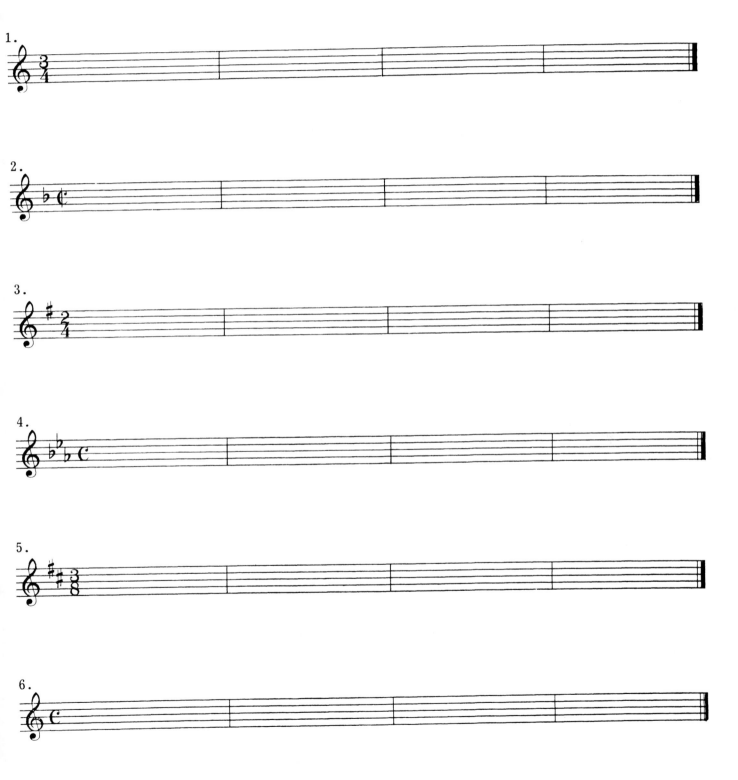

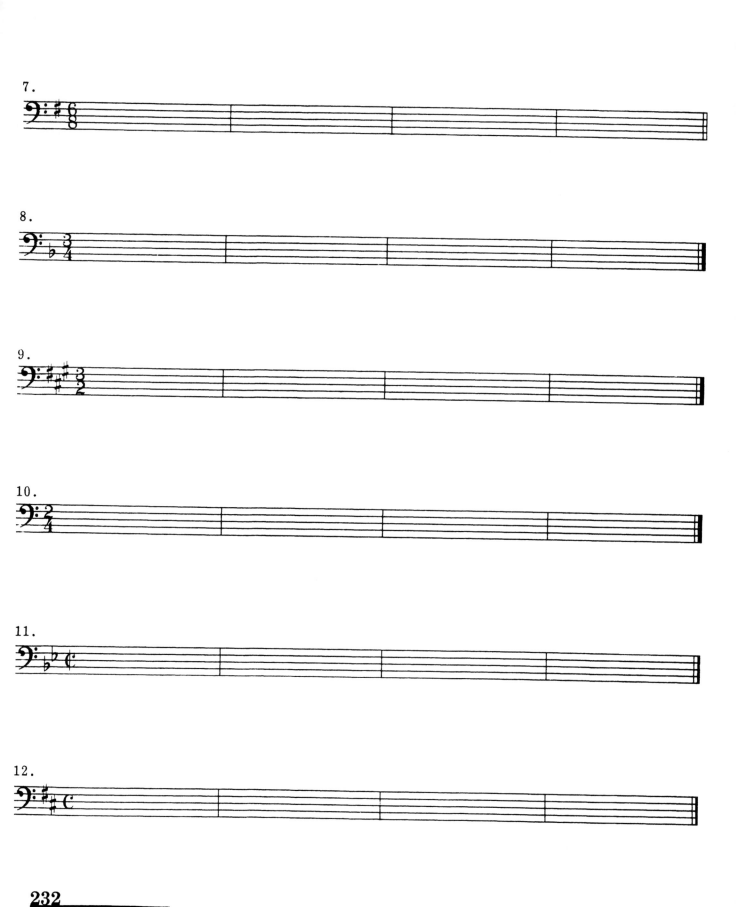

Chromaticism in Major Scales

1. C Major

2. B♭ Major

3. D Major

4. A♭ Major

Chromaticism in minor Scales

1. c minor

2. d minor

3. b♭ minor

4. b minor